RUNNING ON EMPTY?

My dearest Peggy,
This book saved me. I thought it is a... wish everyone would read it. Bless you in all you do.
Love,
Karina
Christmas 2010.

Running on Empty?

A Practical Guide to a Contented Life

Joseph Burns Alston

CFI
Springville, Utah

© 2008 Joseph Burns Alston
All rights reserved.

No part of this book may be reproduced in any form whatsoever, whether by graphic, visual, electronic, film, microfilm, tape recording, or any other means, without prior written permission of the publisher, except in the case of brief passages embodied in critical reviews and articles.

This is not an official publication of The Church of Jesus Christ of Latter-day Saints. The opinions and views expressed herein belong solely to the author and do not necessarily represent the opinions or views of Cedar Fort, Inc. Permission for the use of sources, graphics, and photos is also solely the responsibility of the author.

ISBN 13: 978-1-59955-106-7

Published by CFI, an imprint of Cedar Fort, Inc., 2373 W. 700 S., Springville, UT, 84663
Distributed by Cedar Fort, Inc., www.cedarfort.com

LIBRARY OF CONGRESS CATALOGING-IN-PUBLICATION DATA

Alston, Burns.
 Running on empty / Burns Alston.
   p. cm.
 ISBN 978-1-59955-106-7 (alk. paper)
 1. Christian life--Mormon authors. I. Title.
 BX8656.A47 2007
 248.4'89332--dc22
                            2007040575

Cover design by Nicole Williams
Cover design © 2008 by Lyle Mortimer

Printed in the United States of America

10 9 8 7 6 5 4 3 2 1

Printed on acid-free paper

This book is dedicated to all, especially to those longing for contentment and to ordinary people currently dealing with extraordinary difficulties.

To family and friends first.

From a lover of people—all colors, creeds, and sizes.

Acknowledgments

First, and forever, thank you to my wife and best friend, Karen, for your encouragement and for helping me believe I had something worthwhile to share.

Second, as a school and religion teacher, I have taught thousands of young people. I have also been their student. Thanks to all my children—they have been the real teachers. Our own five children have taught me the most.

Third, you unpaid editors, artists, and other helpers, especially John and Dari—thanks so much.

And finally, please see the last page of this book for a list of some books I cherish. I call them "Hand of God" books. We all need a shelf for such literature. Books can change thoughts, which then change how we traverse and view life. I owe much to good literature. If you do not have your own collection, begin one. Thanks to the many great minds I have tapped for insights. Books are medicine for the soul. May this little book guide your healing and overall sense of contentment.

Contents

Prologue ix
1. Owner's Manual. 1
2. Gas-Guzzling Enemies. 11
3. Steering Your Vehicle 31
4. Enjoying the Journey. 37
5. Listening for Engine Trouble 43
6. Avoiding Dead Ends 49
7. Accidents Happen 55
8. No Worries. 59
9. Traveling My Way 63
10. Approaching Marriage 69
11. LDS Makes and Models 75
12. All Fellow Drivers 81
Epilogue: Arriving at Contentment 85
"Hand of God" Books 88

Prologue

This is just what the world needs—I know—another book on how to live well. But this book is unique. You, yourself, will author the most important, life-altering part of this little book. I will simply be along for the ride. The real work is yours.

You will be required to interact—to actively work out and alter your world where you find the need for course correction.

Let's get one thing straight. Nothing I say is original. I'm not fool enough to bat behind Lou Gehrig or Babe Ruth.

One of the wisest men ever to have lived said it this way: "The thing that hath been, it is that which shall be . . . there is no new thing under the sun" (Ecclesiastes 1:9). Yet, somehow I am naive enough to believe I can say something worthwhile to help you improve your trip.

Perhaps you have seen the movie *Cars*. The animated characters are all vehicles. The theme is that many vehicles are currently on the wrong road for them and perhaps ought to slow down long enough to consider slightly altering their travel plans.

Many men and women are presently living lives of what Henry Thoreau calls "quiet desperation." They are not content with their lot. Thoreau felt that contented people learn to simplify. We must simplify circumstances, needs, wants, and ambitions in order to find the sanity we seek. We must learn to take time to delight in simplicity and nature, ignore some public expectations,

Prologue

refuse to act on the opinions of others, and reject all-too-common definitions of success.

I have been a careful observer of life's lessons, and though I do not wish to sound preachy, I wish to help you improve your gas mileage, and I ache to share insights with you. I believe that just about every other person we interact with is currently struggling with some life challenge—and so I wrote this book.

A favorite author of mine once asked me, "To what song would you set your life trip?" I chose John Lennon's "Imagine." It's a song about peace, but on the whole, the world is not listening to its message.

Are you happy with your present tune? What song would you choose? Are you willing to consider switching music?

Ideas presented herein provide directions for living contently and are especially written for those feeling overwhelmed, tired, confused, or weary of life—those running on empty. This book may provide you with tank-filling directions that limit future feelings of emptiness.

Plato reminds us that the unexamined life is hardly worth living. I know—self-examination can be painful, but it's sometimes necessary. And it's always beneficial.

Socrates felt the beginning of wisdom was an admission of one's own ignorance. I concur. Are you ready to admit your own "not on purpose" ignorance of the past and admit how you have thus failed to live a full life?

Friends ask what my thoughts will be about and I answer, "I write about living a less painful, unhurried, focused life of contentment."

Happiness and contentment are not the same. Happiness is circumstantial—it depends on outside influences that are possibly beyond our control (money, good looks, health, and so on). Contentment, however, has no preconditions. Contentment can be found by all—rich, poor, sick, healthy, bond, free, privileged, and underprivileged. A lifestyle full of joy, in any circumstances, can be acquired. If you lack contentment and feel you could use some refueling, *fill up here*.

Above all else, I am a teacher. And since effective teachers encourage active learning, I will simply facilitate as you work out the answers to your own unique challenges—as you read and write in your own reflections journal within the pages of this book. Feel free to record your thoughts right here as you read.

Running On Empty? is both a book and a journal. Wise teachers know students have the answers to most questions and if only given time, strategies, direction, and materials, they will eventually puzzle them out.

Many good people are just "too busy" for what lies within these pages. If this is you, do not bother—or maybe you are just the one who needs to read

Prologue

on. You decide, but be warned—given a chance, this little book will cause you to improve your life, will positively influence your way of thinking, and will inspire change. It will alter and enhance your future. It may well become the best money and time you ever spend. Given time, it may even start you on the journey toward lasting contentment.

The story is told of an old rabbi who, when young, wanted to influence the entire world for the better. When middle-aged, he hoped at least to have some positive influence on his community. As years passed, he simply hoped to wisely affect his family. Then, on his deathbed, he simply wished he'd have focused on improving himself—someone he could truly influence for good. Really, only you can change you.

Ever drive past an interesting roadside point of interest and then wish you had stopped? You will benefit from this little book only if you will stop and spend time at points of interest within its pages.

Initially, the book may inflict pain, and I strongly suggest a few hours spent in a solitary place, uninterrupted and alone—just you, a pencil, this book, and your thoughts.

Take me up on a few still hours alone, and the ideas in this book will move you toward a more contented life—a life that feels less purposeless, empty, and overwhelming. A life that is just right. A future that is just enough. A perfect fit. Interact with me and refuel.

What makes me an authority? I witnessed an unusual degree of contentment firsthand via my parents. Example is the best teacher. Perhaps you've never witnessed complete satisfaction personally. That's no one's fault, but it will no longer be an excuse either.

I was raised a member of The Church of Jesus Christ of Latter-day Saints. When understood and lived, its doctrines provide a sense of deep, abiding joyfulness regardless of one's circumstances.

My parents lived lives of what some call "simple abundance." I love this term. They lived in a different, less technologically complicated era, but what they had then, you can capture today—correct principles do not change over time. Learn and apply the arts of contentment.

Your future is my only concern. All royalties from the sale of this book will simply support neurological research.

Though I know advice is seldom universal, if you can set all biases aside, this book will bridge every culture, all faiths, and all socioeconomic differences—all people have the same desires and needs. Herein are presented universal pathways to contentment.

A well-meaning but often misunderstood elderly Buddhist monk wanted to leave his monastery and go off alone to die. Before departing, he was told to leave all he had of worth. He wrote ten wise statements and then vanished. This little book is what I have of worth. May it help direct your paths.

Welcome.

Why I Wrote This Little Book

In our small, Canadian prairie town, I think people see me as a combination of Mr. Baseball, church official, Johnny Appleseed, mountain man, Boy Scout leader, and teacher. The truth is, I know little there is to know about any of these.

But God knows everything. And I am presumptuous enough to think I know something about Him. Because of a life-altering illness, I now see God's influence and presence in everything (even my breakfast cereal). As people's perceptions of God differ slightly, I will henceforth refer to God as our Father. This divine heritage is one that all people have in common.

I believe in miracles and I dare not limit God, but today He has me dying, and I am His most attentive student. Somehow, facing a loss of health sharpens one's vision in life.

I'm a lucky man. I have been handed time with a warning and am surrounded by family who love me. Friends write, drop off "cures," offer to edit my book, and call to take me "fishing." I think I understand how to live and love, and I am presently learning about what people can do without.

I have been an ordinary kind of person. You know, one of those nine-to-five people (yes, teachers do work that long). We are the kind that does most of the world's "real" work. (I know Oprah would agree.) If we ordinary people look back over our walks through life, we do some pretty amazing stuff.

Raised a simple country boy, I grew up swimming in ditches, "stealing" crab apples, and playing street-side sports—before a kid's life became over-programmed.

I became a teacher because I love kids, and while a Christian missionary, spending two years in Japan, I gained an insatiable appetite for witnessing lives change when correct principles were understood. I decided, after several less fulfilling career paths, that effective teaching could change lives—and even our own worlds.

The Church's doctrines run my engine. Nowhere else on earth that I am aware of are love, life purpose, and mercy so profoundly understood. I am indebted to these teachings and to my parents, who lived their religion and thus taught it to me.

I sprinkle my thoughts with powerful references to books—many from the scriptures, as well as thoughts accumulated over the years from a few of this world's great thinkers.

I believe the Bible to be one of the greatest of all books, as it has fostered contentment and direction in many lives. But truth is truth whether it comes from the Bible, Torah, Koran, or wherever. I have learned not to be territorial about truth—not to limit the light in my life.

After marrying, raising five children, serving as a bishop, administering in a public school, and running a few marathons, I felt my athleticism slipping away and finally stood staring a neurologist in the face. At age fifty, I was diagnosed with ataxia, a rare brain disorder where you lose your ability to physically balance yourself.

Presently, I am losing my ability to walk, talk, and see. I was hurried into early "retirement." Life is like that, isn't it? If you want a good laugh, tell God your plans. Now, instead of climbing mountains and running races, I read and write.

Learning to feel contentment in current circumstances is a must. Is this possible? Oh yes, and essential too. It's okay to cry and feel sorry for ourselves now and then, but we must get on with life.

I want this little book to find its way into your hands. In writing it I have my pay. *Running On Empty?* will help modern travelers better understand their life journey. My writings may offend some, but I did not undertake this project to please my neighbor. Are you offended? Do you wish I had dressed my thoughts differently?

My purpose is your good, and these tank-filling thoughts can be of great worth to those who sense their value.

Chapter One

Owner's Manual

*What will you make of yourself in this life?
You only live once, so let's get it right.*

Vehicles come with owner's manuals. *Running On Empty?* could well become your owner's manual for living a life of greater happiness and contentment—the quest of all humankind.

Sometimes it's hard to keep driving, even when all is running reasonably well. What do I do when I see an engine light or feel a breakdown coming?

A friend of mine, who has had a few breakdowns of his own, including illness and the unexpected death of a son, on hearing of my life-shortening diagnosis, wisely counseled, "Go right through the middle."

Life is supposed to be hard. (I know it still hurts.) But I am convinced that post-9/11 New York is stronger now, and New Orleans will rise better than before.

Lance Armstrong reportedly said of his cancer that it was his chance to get strong. That's the attitude! It seems humans can be their best when times are worst.

No matter how well tuned up we think we are, breakdowns happen. People get sick and accidents occur. I ate well, exercised, ran on premium gas, and yet I am where I am—disabled. Even a Mercedes or a Cadillac can leave its owner stranded.

I am here to encourage you to stay on the road. Hold on to hope. There may be a few gas stations you've been missing along your way. Perhaps this manual can point them out.

You may be running pretty much on empty right now, but you are not entirely drained, or you would not be reading. The fact that you picked up this book is evidence that you want to improve your driving skills.

Despite all of the tragedies in our world, I believe a loving God is in control. You may not feel this in your present situation, but I am convinced that God doesn't play dice—God plays chess. Your life has purpose. Your struggles have meaning. Your life and your struggles are no accident.

One day I received a visit from my friend Rodger. I coached him in high school baseball many years ago, and we knew each other fairly well, so I suppose he felt he could visit. Rodger was having a few troubles of his own, so there was plenty to discuss. Recently, he had lost three family members, was scheduled for open-heart surgery, and had separated from his wife with the inevitability of divorce.

"I hope you're not giving up," I began.

"No, I haven't quit," Rodger replied.

"Quitting isn't an option," I said.

"Oh, I'm okay," Rodger responded.

"Liar," I said, grinning. "Let's talk real."

We did "talk real," and his pain was obvious. Knowing I really didn't understand but wanting desperately to give him hope, I continued with, "You know, Rodger, though it really doesn't help much now, I think that our roads have strategically placed, individualized bumps and detours needed to help us develop character before our final trip home. Sounds strange, but I believe our unique struggles are part of Father's grand purposes, to teach us some things we need to learn about living and about ourselves. Challenges carry purpose. Life is no accident. Neither is your unique travel log. It's kinda like a tough test we'd rather not have to take, but it's compulsory for everyone before graduation. Eventually, something happens to us all."

As a bishop, having tried to help members of my own faith survive divorce, I knew a bad breakup could drive one to the psych ward—or worse—and a person needed to reach out. So, further feeling him out, I said, "I am so sorry, but I need to say something to make sure you really are okay."

"Sure," Rodger responded.

"Some people are tempted to intentionally shortcut their trips. This is never a wise option and will not impress Father. In fact, though I do not minimize your pain, I believe cutting short one's trip to be one of the most selfish acts humanly possible. Are you this desperate? Any dark thoughts?" I asked.

"No, it hurts to lose family," he replied, "but I'll be okay in time."

I was satisfied that he meant what he had said. Divorced or not, Rodger had children who needed him.

Looking him straight in the eye, I said, "Rodger, I don't want to know details. But it may help you to realize that hurt people hurt people. It is really not all your doing. But I do have a second concern. As a schoolteacher, I have learned something of the pain children of divorced parents experience." Out of concern for his kids, I continued. "Whatever you do, Rodger, do not cause your family more pain by badmouthing their other half. You will always be their dad, and she will always be their mom. Instead, think, *What legacy will I now leave my children?* There's still a future, and your future legacy will live on and will be remembered. This is a turning point for you where you may grow up and realize the core of strength that is in you. You can and must survive this pain."

Skeptics say, "Why would a loving God make life so hard—allow such hardship and trial?" Larry King recently asked this of a panel of today's leading religionists. They were stumped. I wanted to shout, "Read the book of Job!" But I doubt they'd have heard. These men obviously had not yet encountered life-shaking trials. Job said, "Man is born unto trouble, as [sure as] sparks fly upwards" (Job 5:7). It's going to happen. It's even supposed to happen.

Our Father allows struggles because He gives us opportunities to develop Godlike attributes even though it is often terribly painful. It's kind of like disciplining your own child in order to prepare them for their future lives. So, "despise not thou the chastening of the Lord" (Hebrews 12:5). Like a trusting child, we may not completely understand now, but one day we'll see the wisdom of a loving, wise parent.

My brother studied at Harvard. I recall a discussion he once had with fellow students, which he then related to me. He was defending a social value viewed as rather old-fashioned today. His classmates insisted there were no absolute truths (good enough reason for me to avoid too much intellectualism). My brother's experience reminds me of a scripture in the Book of Mormon: "O the vainness, and the frailties, and the foolishness of men! When they are learned they think they are wise" (2 Nephi 9:28).

I couldn't disagree with these "intellectuals" more. There are certain universal truths—absolutes, if you will—that all rational human beings need to someday accept if they are ever to find a contented life. These absolutes, when understood and accepted, make this brief trip through life purposeful and even enjoyable.

The story is told of Einstein carefully building a functioning model of our solar system, complete with its numerous, varied rotations. His purpose in organizing this model was to convince his atheistic friend that God exists. Prior to his friend's entering the room, Einstein carefully set his model in motion. His friend was astounded by the model's beauty, intricacy, and precision.

Einstein's friend asked him, "Who built this?"

Einstein curtly replied, "No one; it simply showed up."

Did you know there are over fifty billion known stars? Is this just some big accident?

Admiral Byrd, after five months of scientific study alone in the Antarctic, concluded that he could feel no doubt of man's oneness with the universe. He had a feeling that transcended reason. He realized that nature's rhythm was too orderly to be the product of chance. His reason said that man's despair was senseless, and he found it groundless.

No matter which religion you follow or don't follow, for those who seek truth, the world's greatest minds conclude that there is endless evidence of an all-powerful intelligence.

To those who ask if I have seen God, I reply, "Not yet, but I have not seen my own spirit either and I know it exists."

"I don't know if you believe in your Heavenly Father, Rodger," I said during our visit. "But some things in life, we just can't handle alone. Like divorce, rejection, or terminal illness, and we need to trust Father is in His heaven; He cares for us. Just keep driving, giving your troubles and pains to Him. I call giving Father our pains 'kissing it up to God.'"

The self-declared atheist who denies both God and miracles is sorely misled. Any reasonable, nonreligious scientist would have to admit that the very brain that allows such a thought is indeed a miracle.

And, ladies, I also happen to believe Father has an equally creative, powerful spouse. You don't take second place in any way.

I didn't tell Rodger all that I wanted to for concern it might be too much, but this is how I view life. This is what I would like to have told Rodger . . .

1. Where did we come from?

It has been said that our physical birth is a spiritual death and our physical death will be a spiritual birth. I like this analogy. You can't make something of nothing. We had to have existed in some way before birth.

I sometimes think of Father as a great fire or beacon of light. People are candles lit by this source of light—born of heavenly parents. Peering into a child's eyes, it is evident God is "the Father of lights" (James 1:17).

Because we are the offspring of heavenly parents—their children—they care about each of us, even though we may not presently feel this concern. Heavenly parents know who you are even if you do not feel cared for. You once existed with them before this life. They care no matter how much you have abused your vehicle, no matter what roads you have or have not taken, or which traffic laws you have ignored.

Too many people are guilt-driven. No matter what errors or troubles you may have encountered, nothing gives you the right to limit Father's love, forgiveness, or willingness to help you now.

You are heaven's miracle creation, and you cannot put a dent in your heavenly parents' love—their love is unconditional.

Notice what happens when good parents are disappointed: "Thou art angry, O Lord, with this people, because they will not understand thy mercies" (Alma 33:16).

If you have heretofore been taught to fear God, your teacher does not understand Father's true character. To fear God simply means to respect and reverence Him. After all, "God is love" (1 John 4:16).

Oprah interviewed actor Matthew McConaughey as 2005's sexiest man of the year. What appealed to most viewers, besides Matthew's good looks, was his obvious self-confidence and self-assurance. When asked why he appeared so comfortable in his own skin, he answered, "I am a child of God."

Oprah was somewhat stunned. The audience applauded. At some level, they sensed this truth.

Some of you may feel that a God who loves you is just too hokey. But I believe all things witness of God. "All things denote there is a God; yea, even the earth, and all things that are upon the face of it, yea, and its motion, yea, and also all the planets which move in their regular form do witness that there is a Supreme Creator" (Alma 30:44).

Many talk of gaining self-esteem. Accepting where you came from, your inherited goodness, and that you are a heavenly, deliberate creation—God's child—is your lasting source of self-esteem, the premium-octane gas to keep you traveling contentedly. You are a child of God and therefore are inherently of great worth.

2. *Why are we here?*

Life is messy, but despite your messes, you were born to be content. Epictetis was a poor, lame slave in Nero's Rome. He believed that if a man is unhappy, his unhappiness is his own fault, because God made everyone to be happy.

In the Book of Mormon we read, "Men are, that they might have joy" (2 Nephi 2:25). The truly happy, contented man is a believer—an optimist. No pessimist I know of ever discovered anything worthwhile.

When things go wrong, as they sometimes will, when the road you travel feels all uphill, rest or cry but do not quit. Life's road has its twists and turns, as every one of us eventually learns. But you might just win if you stick it out.

Cry alone a little, then turn on the wipers. Get up and remember you really are Father's child and are therefore inherently tougher than this. Forget about your culture and what anybody thinks or says you should be. Remember, your worth is inherent—not earned.

To help you find contentment, to bump into joy and get on the road again, you will need to stop being "a real go-getter" and instead become "a real go-giver." Sounds corny, but you must align yourself with some cause for social good.

Contentment is not found in being. Contentment is not found in having. Contentment is found in doing—doing for others. Contentment involves a bit of self-forgetting.

Renowned author and Auswitch concentration camp survivor Victor Frankl, in *Man's Search for Meaning*, relates how he survived his imprisonment. He said it was by choosing to share his last crust of bread. He could choose his own path, and no influence could take from him his God-given ability to choose how he'd act in any set of circumstances. In his story we find a profound lesson.

Ironic, I know, but to fill your own tank, you must learn to share your fuel, not hoard it. Someone said that service is the rent we pay for the space we take up in this world. No one ought to ride the bus without contributing in some way.

The older I get the more I realize that life and God are full of apparent contradictions. Small kindling makes the best fire, people are healed (if they'll allow) by their own wounds, and contentment comes through giving. I also find that the closer we get to being God-like, the more we enjoy the company of ordinary people. I see now why truly great men and women prefer the company of the poor, needy, and outcast.

The details of how to capture contentment or OK-ness are unique to everyone, but it is always done by first accepting who you are, and then by caring for others. "When ye are in the service of your fellow beings ye are only in the service of your God" (Mosiah 2:17).

Truly loving ourselves, and then serving others that may be running on empty, is the great secret in all of our travels. This is how we help pump gas.

Do not allow anything hurtful or comfortable to distract you from the knowledge of your divine nature and your obligation to serve your fellow travelers. Even in my present limited circumstances, I can find small ways to brighten someone's path.

Life can be depressing, but that's life. If you have problems, don't assume there is something defective in you or your heavenly parents. Struggling with challenge is at the core of life. Our creators have not made some mistake. They are givers of good gifts only. Try not to confuse the expected good and the given good. Content souls learn to trust the giver more than the gift while continuing to give good gifts of their own.

Your heavenly parents use pain and struggle as a chance for you to become more like them—to prove you bitter or better. They made both pain and pleasure to teach us.

When your road gets bumpy, remember this is part of your journey. It will not last long. Ask yourself, am I allowing life to make me better? If so, your pain is, ironically, a blessing. "Let us run with patience the race that is set before us" (Hebrews 12:1).

Throughout history, great minds have concluded that it is the difficult that most instructs. So, as strange as it may seem, the wise will not dread but, rather, will grow, even learning to embrace their struggles.

Why do our heavenly parents want us to grow? What are we growing toward? For answers, we turn to the Bible: "Let this mind be in you, which was also in Christ Jesus: Who being in the form of God, thought it not robbery to be equal with God" (Philippians 2:5–6).

What will you make of yourself in this life? We only live once, so let's get it right.

I do not understand why so many in our world cannot accept our becoming God-like. We are God's children. A baby chicken does not become a horse.

Life has its perplexing problems, but I assure you there is purpose. Use your pain to help fellow travelers—that is precisely what God did for us. Trust that Father will help you here and, I promise you, He will make it all more than fair in the end. "He shall consecrate thine afflictions for thy gain" (2 Nephi 2:2).

We are reminded, "All things wherewith you have been afflicted shall work together for your good" (D&C 98:3). To endure your challenges you would do well to develop, and regularly practice, spirit-building rituals that meet your own unique life circumstances.

To simply prescribe scripture study, prayer, or attending church on Sunday as everyone's complete path to healing is presumptuous indeed. Although many of these rituals have proven themselves over time, you will need to find what strengthens you spiritually. Your journey takes personal planning and is yours alone.

If you are 35 now and live to 75, you have 480 months left on this planet. That's if you're lucky enough to get that far. Many of us have less time. Do your own math.

A "wake up" verse for me captures why people are here: "This life is the time . . . to prepare to meet God; . . . the day of this life is the day . . . to perform their labors" (Alma 34:32).

Though difficult to accept, health is simply the longest route to death. Father's "horn," with which He gets our attention, is pain. Some days we may wish His horn were silent.

People who never accept who they are and that life is meant to be hard fill life with *fluff*—stuff that doesn't last. Remember, what matters most is what lasts longest. Isaiah said, "Wherefore do ye spend money for that which is not bread [doesn't last]? and your labour for that which satisfieth not?" (Isaiah 55:2).

Each of us will give our life to something—a career, a sport, money, a conviction, people, and so forth. What will you focus on? For what or who will you live? I suggest you write answers in your "reflections journal" right here.

3. Where are we going?

Eventually, all vehicles end up in a scrap yard. All people end up in a cemetery. It has been said that we should not become too attached to this life because no one gets out alive. Earth life is fatal. Death is a vehicle parked outside every home. Not to sadden you, but sooner or later you must go for a ride. As death is inevitable, and we each must confront this one day, this topic deserves our attention.

I believe all people, at some point, experience a yearning for a spiritual home. Like memories of a cherished vehicle you once owned, part of you lives on long after your car has been traded in.

Your unbelief won't change the truth—we all travel back to that God who gave us life. "The spirits of all men [and women and children], as soon as they are departed from this mortal body, yea, the spirits of all men, whether they be good or evil, are taken home to that God who gave them life" (Alma 40:11).

God wants you to succeed while here—to experience contentment despite adversity.

Compared to the eternal road that we are traveling, this life is simply a brief pit stop along the way. We only do a few laps no matter how long we live. I've heard life compared to a dream, a small moment, even a burp.

Don't make yourself too much at home on life's highway. We are all just visitors here, "strangers and pilgrims on the earth" (Hebrews 11:13).

We were born to die. We will never feel entirely content in this life because we feel a certain incompleteness here—we lived elsewhere before and we long for home. Just as the Hebrews did, we "desire a better country" (Hebrews 11:16).

One day your heart will quit. The good news is, just as surely as you understand this, I know death will not be the end of your existence. Like the children in C. S. Lewis's *The Lion, the Witch, and the Wardrobe* who enter a wardrobe and find themselves in a world unperceived by most, strangers in a new land, you will enter death simply to live again.

We share a common destination in mortality but the journey, well, that is entirely up to you.

What really matters is, each of us will one day kneel before Father and give an accounting of how navigated our roads here. What will you report? Did you quit? Were your roads just too bumpy? Or, despite your own challenging traffic, did you stop and give a lift to struggling hitchhikers? Were you too busy speeding by?

Loving heavenly parents want you to pass this post–earth life interview. No matter what your faith, the questions will revolve around two relationships. Did you love God and love thy neighbor as thyself (Matthew 22:37–39)?

At your death, rest assured you will not be leaving home—you will be arriving home.

Meanwhile, God requires that we confront our personal pain. Without pain we could never learn our lessons in this life. Heavenly parents will honor our suffering and, one day, though it may seem terribly unfair now, all injustices and pains will be made right. God will help you even now. If allowed, He will "succor his people [that's everyone!] according to their infirmities" (Alma 7:12).

"Now no chastening for the present seemeth to be joyous, but grievous: nevertheless afterward it yieldeth the peaceable fruit of righteousness unto them which are exercised thereby" (Hebrews 12:11).

We increase physical muscle by enduring stress. We increase spirit muscle by learning from, and enduring well, our struggles.

Sarah Flower Adams wrote the well-known hymn "Nearer, My God, to Thee." This hymn was sung as the *Titanic* slowly sank. It is often bearing our own crosses that brings us nearer to God.

Endless metaphors have been used to describe what life is like. My favorite, as you can tell, is a vehicle (us) on a journey (life) down a road (experiences and choices) to our final destination (death and then more life).

Remember that, to a large degree, you are driving. Some people actually believe life is just what happens to them. Not so, though some things do just seem to happen.

I may not even know you, but my heartfelt wish is that you never give up. It is easy to feel lost and alone in this world. But God is awake and watching over your course.

I enjoy earth life, but I also agree with the following perspective on this existence. "The only difference between the old and young dying is, one lives longer in heaven and eternal light . . . than the other, and is freed a little sooner from this miserable wicked world."[1]

I find constant refueling and thoughtful preparation before any trip to be invaluable. It may sound bold but, regardless of who you are, without accepting and trusting the principles in this owner's manual you will never be completely content while here.

You may find that the answers to the big questions are a real reach for you, but I can assure you that we arrive at true wisdom and contentment when we accept not only what we can understand, but what we comprehend fully only with our hearts.

I would like to have taught these truths to Rodger, but we were both tiring, so he wished me well and was off.

Before he left, he gave me his new phone number and email address and said, "Let's stay in touch. And I will pray for you."

I believe he will, and I will be thinking of him as I pray.

"Do you mind if I make us laugh before you go?" I asked.

Rodger replied, "Why not?"

"There was a wife in a grocery store caught stealing and her husband was a witness. They found themselves in front of a judge who asked what she had stolen. The husband testified that his wife had stolen a can of peaches. The judge asked her how many slices were in the can and then assigned her one day in the slammer per slice. Upon hearing this verdict, the husband quickly proceeded to inform the judge that she had also stolen a can of peas."

Until our trials, Rodger and I had only talked baseball. I had a feeling that when he'd somewhat recovered from his open-heart surgery, we would do some more "real talking."

Notes
1. Joseph Smith, *Teachings of the Prophet Joseph Smith*, Joseph Fielding Smith, comp. Salt Lake City: Deseret Book, 197.

Chapter Two

Gas-Guzzling Enemies

*We have to decide what to do
with the time that is given to us.*

The doorbell rang and though a bit soon after open-heart surgery, I thought it might be Rodger, so I yelled, "Come in."

My wife, Karen, and I were pleasantly surprised when a long-time friend entered.

"I haven't seen you forever," Juli said.

"We don't get around much anymore," I replied, and the look in her eye told me she understood.

We made our way to our reflective, oriental yoga room Karen had created in our comfortable home and started chatting.

After some polite small talk, Juli expressed a concern she was struggling with. She seemed most concerned about life's frantic pace. Like most people, life was just so hectic for her. I admired her for reaching out and not pretending.

Our conversation went something like this.

"I just don't seem to have any time," Juli said.

I thought to myself, *We all have the same number of minutes in a day*, but I wisely kept this to myself. The next words she spoke had a lasting impact on me.

"I only get one chance at this life, you know—and this is no dress rehearsal."

She is so right.

The story is told of a Northern Canadian who owned land and a pond.

Each year migratory birds rested on his little lake while heading south. Winter came early. The lake froze over and unexpected accidents occurred as birds attempted their landings.

The landowner knew the solution but, like most quick, nonreflective decisions, he was dead wrong. In the scriptures we read, "You must study it out in your mind" (D&C 9:8).

He called his friend (home for the weekend from working in the oil patch) and said, "Help me out and bring a stick of dynamite."

The landowner picked up his buddy. They drove to the lake in his new truck. In the back, his hunting hound barked approval at the prospect of the upcoming excursion.

"We'll just blast a hole," the frustrated owner said as he watched a few unsuspecting fowl ricochet off the ice.

As instructed, his buddy lit the stick and then tossed it onto the lake's surface.

Imagine their surprise when the dog jumped from the rear of the truck to retrieve the "stick." Proud of his prize, the dog began trotting back to his owner, who was seated in the shiny new truck. Frantically, the dog's owner did what he thought was his only option—he dove for the gun behind his seat and began firing feverishly at the dog in an attempt to halt his return. He missed. The dog spooked and fled to safety underneath the pickup. *Kaboom.* The rest is history. I doubt the car insurance company covered stupidity.

Though shocked by what transpired in this story—we are not so very different. We may think there is a quick, simple, nonreflective right answer to our problems. Wrong. Life's frozen ponds deserve careful pondering, weighing all options before carelessly proceeding. Ever tried pondering before now? It's time.

People simply do not take the time necessary to solve life's problems. It is not that we don't have the answers. It's that we don't take the time. Scott Peck, a world famous psychologist and author of *The Road Less Traveled*, understood this truth. We need to take the time necessary to analyze problems so as to develop well-thought-out and effective solutions (your purpose in reading this book). Problems don't simply go away.

Like a well-running vehicle, we have to be tuned up regularly or eventually we have a breakdown.

For every life problem there is a quick, easy, wrong answer.

Until we stop ignoring our problems, we will never come up with proper solutions. Have you accepted that you need to stop ignoring your problems? What is it that you need to focus on? Maybe it remains unclear. Try to put it in words here.

At least capturing it on paper gives you a chance for a solution.

Let's return to my conversation with our friend Juli.

"Juli, your challenge has an answer, but it requires quiet, reflective time—the very commodity you feel short of," I replied.

Had our landowner quietly considered all options carefully, his day would likely have turned out differently. Was dynamite really the only way? What if he had left his dog home? Did he really need him? Was shooting his dog truly his only choice? Think about it.

Well, he suffered the consequences of his hurried choices, and, similarly, we suffer for our own unexamined lives.

Our story could have had a much happier ending—like our lives—had possible "enemies" been identified.

Just as the dog hid under the truck to avoid gunfire, we too hide behind a whole pickup load of deceptions we desperately hope (even believe) will bring contentment. But they let us down—and results can be devastating.

There a several key enemies of a life full of joy. First and foremost is busyness (you know, the I'm-in-a-hurry syndrome). Next on the list is what I call buying into our culture's counterfeit praise (seeking the shallow approval of others). Finally, we come to misunderstanding the importance (better yet, the unimportance) of money and material things. Until these three gasoline guzzlers are confronted and effectively resolved, you will not get great mileage.

I didn't get to tell this to Juli because she seemed to be in a hurry. But I am confident that if you will spend some reflective time with this chapter and your unhurried thoughts, you can make major progress on your road to greater contentment.

Our purpose is to engage the enemies in battle—a fight for your future. Busyness, counterfeit praise, and material things, though temporarily distracting and gratifying, carry with them a lingering sense of emptiness, a sense that there must be more—and there is. Much more. If you disagree, you are deceiving yourself. It is so easy to be fooled. We have all been there and are still stuck there to some degree.

The following are true principles an everyday person like you and me can apply in our lives to empower us, simplify things, and enable us to direct this one life we each live.

I draw upon ordinary experiences. My future and my own look at life's brevity have crystallized life's priorities.

There is no arguing that what you are about to read—if applied—will bring you a refillable joy and abundance. These universal truths will refill your tank. Be bold.

Of people's lives it could be said, "There are many called, but few are chosen. And why are they not chosen? Because their hearts are set so much upon the things of this world, and aspire to the honors of men" (D&C 121:34–35).

Just as surely as our world's petroleum shortages will one day result in a world energy crisis, if you do not stop, if you do not address these major gas guzzling enemies, and you do not identify meaningful alternate energy sources, you too will end up in crisis.

The following are travel tips to help you keep that tank full, no matter how hectic traffic becomes.

Enemy #1—Busyness

A teenage cancer victim reportedly wrote this poem.

Slow Dance

Have you ever watched kids on a merry-go-round?
Or listened to the rain just slapping on the ground?
Ever followed a butterfly's erratic flight?
Or gazed at the sun into the fading night?
You'd better slow down. Don't dance so fast.
Time is short, and the music won't last.

Do you run through each day on the fly?
When you ask, "How are you?" do you even hear the reply?
When the day is done, do you lie in bed with a hundred things to do running
    through your head?
You'd better slow down. Don't dance so fast.
Time is short, and the music won't last.

Ever told a child "We'll do it tomorrow"?
Then, in your haste, not noticed the sorrow?
Ever lost touch and let a good friendship die?
'Cause you never had time to call and say, "Hi."
You'd better slow down. Don't dance so fast.
Time is short, and the music won't last.

When you run so fast trying to get somewhere, you miss the fun of getting there. When you hurry and worry throughout your day, it is like an unopened gift . . . just thrown away.

Life is not a race. Do take it slower and, please, hear the music before the song is over.

Time is the stuff life is made of, and it will be the proper managing of this commodity that largely determines whether your tank feels full or empty.

We have to decide what to do with the time that is given us. Ever felt thin, like too little butter spread over too much toast, like you are running near empty?

This is what drove Henry D. Thoreau into the solitude of the woods. There he concluded that most people lead lives of what he called quiet desperation.

Many of us feel too busy, too overwhelmed, to address our struggles, so we choose to ignore them—to continue our lives of quiet desperation rather than expend the time and mental energy needed to actually switch directions. It can be frightening, but one definition of insanity is repeatedly doing what we already know won't work. Ever feel a bit insane?

Your time is your responsibility. It is ultimately up to you alone to decide how you use and order your time. The consequences are your responsibility. You are entirely free to choose to structure your time differently. So quit complaining about being so busy. It's your own choice. Instead of complaining, do something about it.

The "hurry-up" life is almost prescribed by our North American culture. I recall setting a New Year's resolution in my early thirties not to hurry or even say the word anymore. At a party, we shared our resolutions, and when I shared mine a hush fell over the crowd—a hush of, "Yes, I feel it too." Especially during holiday seasons. I'm convinced that Father never hurries through times of struggle, even when we wish He would.

An acquaintance of mine living in Taiwan says the Chinese characters making up the word *busy* are a combination of the symbols for *death* and *heart*. The Chinese are right. Too much busyness results in the death of one's heart. Heavenly Father counsels us, "Be still, and know that I am God" (D&C 101:16).

My first indication that I suffered from the "hurry up" syndrome was when I noticed I flushed before finishing my "business."

Then I noticed busyness all around me. It occurred to me how much women reminded me of a Chinese juggling acrobat I once saw while vacationing in Florida. He had nothing on many women I know. Ladies are remarkable. They can eat, clean the house, and talk on the phone all at the same time.

While waiting at a doctor's office, women can do their stretches, make the day's to-do list, and read a magazine, simultaneously. Our culture calls it multitasking. I call it exhausting.

Three capable, put-together women friends of ours recently told me in their own ways that they feel like they are "on a treadmill and can't get off." Even those who seem to have everything under control may feel frenzied by all of the tasks that fill up their days. Now when I observe people's hectic pace, I want to shout, "Change lanes!"

One of my all-time favorite denunciations of unnecessary busyness came from Christ himself when he told Martha not to be so "cumbered about [with] serving" (Luke 10: 38–42) and instead to take time, listen, and acknowledge His presence.

Our busy culture does not make people feel good about themselves or foster lasting relationships—things that result in contentment. You have to learn to be strong enough to monitor your speed. Go ahead and defy your culture. It is refreshing.

A man I admire took his wife and children camping all summer. He escaped his culture and created some of his family's most cherished memories.

A younger, hardworking farmer recently spoke in church on working less and spending more time on things that last (relationships). I wonder, was his recent heart attack a coincidental trial or his chance to really enjoy and enhance life?

I do value hard work, but even work must be managed. There must be an underlying, deeper purpose even in our labor. Too often we make a living but fail to live. Cold and hunger are less frightening than the means we sometimes employ to meet these basic needs.

The world is a place of business (and busyness). It is work, work, and work.

Another young friend of mine just selected his profession. I applaud his reasoning behind his choice of career. It is because he will not have to work Fridays. He is making his living and carving out time to play.

I love to see people playing. Work is a necessary part of our busyness, but too often it is directly opposed to real living. Work as little as you can. Do you really want to spend life hoarding money and then leaving it for others to spend? Or will you be unique?

Many people walk around with their gas tanks close to empty. They seem alert but allow work to drive them. They get good things done but spend little on the essential. Trust me, an accident is waiting to happen.

Often I sense confusion within the culture of my own faith. I often hear well-meaning people say family comes first. This is false. Even spouses let each other down. Truth and God never change loyalties. To capture contentment, place your loyalty in truth first. "And ye shall know the truth, and the truth shall make you free" (John 8:32).

Next, focus on family, with your spouse topping the list; then focus on making a living. Get these out of order and a day of accountability waits.

I am a teacher, and, though my students won the provincial title in spelling three times, I say children and spouses spell *love* T-I-M-E. If you ever feel like you just need quality time, it's a sure sign you are over committed. Take charge.

The other day I found myself encouraging a close friend. This friend has meaningful employment, wonderful children, and a beautiful home, but is sometimes running on empty. How can this person lack joy?

Remember, happiness is not about your circumstances. I have temporarily lost my health and, though pained, in many ways have never been more content: I am full of love for truth, family, and sincere friends.

Likely your lifestyle is one of over commitment and busyness. You have power to change this. Others, not so concerned, may protest, but you must direct your own life, or the world and others will direct it for you.

As much as I revere truth, I sometimes resent the cultures we create. Truth and culture/tradition are not the same. You've heard of the woman who always cut the end off the pot roast because her mother and grandmother always did. She finally realized it was only because their pots were too small.

Any culture of too much busyness leaves precious little time for meaningful worship and loved ones. Do not dwindle "in unbelief . . . because of the traditions of [your] fathers, which [may] not [be] correct" (Mosiah 1:5).

Our cultures often distract us from contentment. Sometimes the right answer is no. Think in terms of stewardships, and then carefully choose yes or no.

Organizations to which we belong, even though we may consider them divine, are merely scaffoldings. Organizations must support and deepen our understanding of truth and meaningful, lasting relationships, or they aren't much good to us.

For many years, I had a cartoon hanging on my office wall at school. It depicted two children walking home after a hard day. One boy asks his friend what he is doing that night and if he would like to play. The second boy lists his busy itinerary of lessons, sports, and other commitments and then laments, "I have no time to play."

Many parents today are so busy driving children to lessons and other commitments that they are running near empty. Now, I know our culture says you are a bad parent if you do not conform, but take a giant step backward toward contentment—control your pace. You and yours will benefit—I promise. Of course children need to be involved, but we limited our children to one "extra" activity per season—their choice.

We adults need involvement too—perhaps in church, a social group, or the community. I am not suggesting we live in a cocoon. But in all your involvement, slow down, love, and live.

If you are so rushed that you have no time to love and truly enjoy those with who you associate, you are indeed too busy. In your new future, you must take time to truly enjoy the people in your life.

People must come first in a contented life, and people need unhurried time.

Recently this truth was reinforced one evening as a church youth group came to our door. They had been asked to do some small service for those they called on. Since I am disabled now, there was plenty they could do for us. Just as we were about to respond, one well-meaning young girl shouted, "Oh, we don't have time for that," and they all ran off. That same night, years ago, a person assigned by our bishop to check in on us stopped by and said, "We are too busy to visit this month, but here are some cookies."

Do not get stuck in the hurry or the meeting syndrome. In the LDS Church we have been counseled to have fewer, more effective meetings—to free up Sundays for families. It has been said that the LDS have a fourteenth article of faith, which states, "We believe in meetings."

Magnify your calling, not your busyness. Personally, I avoid meetings when possible. They are a necessary evil. Worship and family duties win over meetings.

I love the question posed in the December 2005 *Ensign*: "How can we magnify our callings while at the same time following the counsel of Church leaders to reduce and simplify the work?" One response included these rhetorical questions that we can ask ourselves:

> Am I overscheduling individuals or families in my ward? Can we coordinate so that most meetings and activities are held one night a week?
>
> Does a particular meeting or activity encourage members to live the gospel, receive saving ordinances, and prepare for exaltation?
>
> Are we focusing more on the people than on the program?
>
> Have I asked the individuals and families I serve or direct what kind of activities would best serve their needs, or am I promoting my own needs and pursuing my own personal agenda?
>
> Do I count the success of the meeting or activity by how many people attended or, rather, by the effect it had on those who did attend?
>
> Does a particular meeting or activity interfere with the family dinner hour?[1]

If you lack contentment in any stewardship, you would do well to ponder these questions.

We are counseled to reduce and to simplify. Yet we make more handouts and fuss too much over the "center pieces" in life, thus heightening our own stress levels.[2]

What is your children's image of you today? Ask them. Hopefully it will be the image of quiet, unhurried time and contentment. They are watching. You may think you are spending these quiet hours with this little book just for yourself, but your reflections are much bigger than just you.

I now have "email Mondays" since I don't get around much anymore. I ask our five children life's many questions. I've noticed some weeks they are too busy to reply meaningfully. The culture is winning. Recently, I asked them for the name of a book that had helped them become a better human being. One had read Victor Frankl's *Man's Search for Meaning*. Another cited Mitch Albom's *Tuesdays with Morrie*. Good for them.

From this point in my life, I often ask them what great mind they are tapping into by reading. If they answer that they are just too busy to be reading some great piece of literature, I will know they truly are too busy. It is another sign.

You are too busy if you have no time to read. Make time to treasure up truth—I believe wisdom is one of God's gifts that goes with us, along with memories of those we love. The scriptures teach, "Whatever principle of intelligence we attain unto in this life, it will rise with us" (D&C 130:18).

A maxim that greatly helps me engage the enemies is this:

People first
Principles second
Programs (busyness) last—dead last

Memorize it. Where is most of your time spent? Likely on programs—on busyness. Too often we focus on the program—the showiness or even a principle or policy—almost completely missing the people.

A young couple entered their bishop's office. They were unemployed and the children were hungry. Is this the time to teach the principle of self-reliance? Certainly not. People first. There would be a time to teach principles and use programs. But not now. Timing priorities is crucial. Solomon knew this when he said, "To every thing there is a season and a time to every purpose under the heaven" (Ecclesiastes 3:1).

Mix up what I call the Three *P*s, and eventually you will crash, and unfortunately you may take some innocent victims with you.

God cares less about what you do than why you do it. To be content, all we do must be grounded in love. Slow down. Loving people is your source of joy.

A daughter and her dad went for a walk one starlit evening. As they held hands, she looked up into her father's eyes and asked, "Dad, what's the most important thing?" He thought a moment then wisely replied with just one word—"Relationships."

I have been honored to spend my last moments here on earth with many. Not once did they mention programs, projects, or productivity. Invariably it was about relationships. I believe strongly that, when we meet Him again, what God will want to know is, "How did you treat your significant other?" and, if you were blessed with children, "What was the quality of those relationships?" Everything else will be secondary.

Life is about love. God is love. Forgiving and loving God, self, and others is the summum bonum of life.

Loving takes time. It is the best use of life. Make time now.

I have concluded that what we take with us at the end of our roads is relationships, character, and wisdom. Focus on these. They alone lead to the contented life.

If you need to rearrange your time, if your relationships are broken or temporarily out of order, repair as best you can. Then move on down your road at a saner pace. Your future contentment is at stake.

As I approach the rest of life, I am done with so-called important things, plans, institutions, and big success. Instead, I am for a slower pace and relationships.

Were I physically able once more, I would use time even more precisely. I would consider hiring out the yard work to a fatherless youth who needs money and being his or her mentor, watching less mindless TV, spending more time (through books) with the great minds of the past, and spending more of life's real currency (time) talking to and sharing my loving humanness.

A goal or direction unwritten is only a wish. Write your reflections. They're your tangible road map for your future.

Julis of the world, hurry is archenemy number one. Unaddressed, this will always be barrier to your contentment.

To gain most from our discussion, reflect on the questions below and take time to answer in this journal.

Tune-Up Time

What are the 3 enemies of contentment, in order?

Over the next six months, what busyness will you eliminate? (Be true to previous commitments. Your integrity matters.)

In your future, to what will you answer no, in order to give time to yourself and your loved ones?

How will you focus newfound time with the people you love? What will you do differently?

Are you guilty of multitasking? What will you stop and do to help fill yourself instead?

What piece of literature have you been longing to read and finally will? (If you need a starting point, try anything by Robert Fulghum.)

Enemy #2—Counterfeit praise

Most people love praise—it's natural, but you must not allow counterfeit praise to occupy any truly important space within you, or lasting contentment will be under attack. Beware of false flattery.

True, in the workplace and in your communities there are those who genuinely appreciate your efforts and are sincere in what they both say and feel.

But what most say or think of you must run off like rain off your windshield. Politely thank well-meaning acquaintances and move on.

A man I admire set as one of his life goals to avoid the false flattery of well-meaning friends. He understood that God gets all the credit. When praise gets inside, contentment is threatened. What most think, simply must not matter. Remember, "pride goeth before destruction" (Proverbs 16:18).

One day a teacher came to the office. Early in the year she had been in desperate need of a leave of absence. Living in a small town where people talk, she told me that if she were on sick leave, she'd feel stress at even leaving the house because of what people may say about her not being at work. She had revealed the source of much of her anxiety. I did not want to be cynical, but I asked her how many of those people she thought really cared.

In regard to who comes first in your life (whose praise counts), use, as a guiding maxim, something I once heard and have never forgotten: "Who will cry when I die?" Surprise! Not many, and certainly not most, of your acquaintances.

Though optimistic that a better day will come, I believe the chief malady of our day to be a lack of taking time to show we care.

People don't care enough to obey God, to really understand Him, and people don't care enough about themselves and others.

Sure, there are plenty of distractions. Busyness, praise of man, and the pursuit of money all get in our way. However, the day must come when we sincerely care more deeply.

A young female colleague of mine woke one snowy Alberta morning, set out driving to school, and died on a highway. I hung by my desk a copy of her obituary to remind me to live my life caring—but not about what others think.

Most office affairs are the direct result of internalized counterfeit praise (caring what non-criers, those who won't cry when you die, say and think of you). Eventually, your shallow admirer will not only not cry but may actually disdain you. We read, "They themselves shall be despised by those that flattered them" (D&C 121:20).

Think about it. It's true. The praiser most often simply wants something from you—they seldom really care about your well-being.

Truth is, most of those you are trying to impress are too busy to take time to really care. If you are concerned about what other people think of you—if you compare yourself with others—stop. Instead, wake up and realize how little society thinks about you and how little strangers really care. When you are twenty, you care about what everyone thinks of you. At forty, you quit caring. At sixty, you realize they didn't think or really care about you in the first place.

Even world famous news anchor Dan Rather worked forty-four years for CBS and was fired via a phone call—not even over lunch.

Yes, fortunate souls do find a genuinely caring group of people in life who will be there even when their road gets rocky. I am thankful for this.

Working as a teacher in a small rural town and loving people as a school administrator and Church member, I have been unusually blessed with praying and "crying" friends. If we are extremely fortunate, loving family surrounds us as well. Some of them will cry. Though, too often, even those who "should" cry for us don't. There are tragic roadblocks even in family relations.

Maybe you've heard, "You're fired!" or "I want a divorce." You may have experienced firsthand rejection or abuse even at the hands of should-be criers. I am sorry. But remember, as much as we'd like to, we do not control others.

Sometimes people never receive the genuine praise from those they cherish most. I recall a friend who had been abused as a child and was full of resentment. She was surprised when I counseled her to take a trip. I told her to go see her father, the man who had abused her, and be reconciled. It helped.

Whatever regrettable turns and roadblocks we may have encountered on life's road, a sincere "I'm sorry, please forgive me" or "I forgive you" will nurture healing and bring you added contentment, regardless of other's response.

Care about those who will cry. A sure road to a lack of contentment is to care what everyone thinks. If you need to ignore some counterfeit praise, if you need to say any of the above to your should-be criers, and you can do so from the heart, do it today. Say, "I love you," "I'm sorry, please forgive me," or "I forgive you."

To help capture increased contentment, to who do you need to say what? You may want to pause and write this.

Facing one's own mortality squarely in the face has a way of getting rid of all the fluff. Yesterday I was an "important," "irreplaceable" Church member, teacher, and school administrator—promptly and effectively replaced. Ouch! Sure, no one does it quite like you did, but the job gets done just the same. Don't kid yourself. This world's praise lasts for no one.

My feeling is that if life lacks clear purpose, and that purpose is not larger than myself, it doesn't matter who praises me or if my life is purposeful. It doesn't matter who criticizes me. I know my destination.

Julis of this world, do not be sucked in by counterfeit praise!

Tune-Up Time

Where and from who do you receive false flattery?

Without being cynical, what will you say or think to yourself to keep phony praise outside?

List those who may (take no one for granted) cry when you die.

Have you inadvertently placed principles, programs, and activities ahead of these people? Identify how and write what you will change.

Is there anything you need to say to them? Be honest with yourself.

Enemy #3—Things

Juli, get things in your life in the right place or be prepared to completely miss your ride.

Thoreau believed that plain living and proper thinking results in a more contented life than accumulation and seeking any monetary standard of living—that the real currency in life has little to do with money.

An experiment to legitimize his belief led him to a quiet two-year existence in a cabin of his own construction beside Walden Pond, where he proved how simply one could live contently. Having proven to himself that one could be content with almost nothing, he moved back to town, seeing no further reason for such extreme action.

He wrote that he went to the woods because he wanted to "live deliberately," and see if he could learn what life had to teach, and not, when he died, discover that he had not really lived.

I'm not suggesting we retreat to the woods. But a few quiet hours might do us some good.

Thoreau is right. Goodness and wonder abound; yet much of our life is spent on illusion, a facade—on things. We, and all we presume to possess, are but a flickering candle in the wind—soon extinguished.

I believe the real price we pay in all our buying and selling is figured by how much of our life (in time) this endeavor takes away from living.

I admire Tevye in the play *Fiddler on the Roof*. He loved his daughters more than tradition or culture—more than what anybody thought. He was unhurried and took time to talk with God, often making decisions that were contrary to his own culture. What I admire most is his balance regarding wealth. Yes, he wished he was a rich man, nothing wrong with that, but don't miss the most important words in his song. He says that if wealthy he'd "sit in the synagogue and pray" and "discuss the holy books for hours every day."

There is nothing wrong with having money. It is a love of money more than relationships for which we will pay.

You can do much good with money. But make no mistake—money cannot buy you contentment, lasting relationships, or real security. These only come by constantly remembering who you really are (a child of God) and then sharing yourself with others.

It's great to have money and the things that money can buy, but it's also good to be sure you haven't lost the things that money can't buy—like integrity.

In modern day, Brigham Young, having led his followers across an unfriendly, trial-laden trail, finally reached his destination—the Salt Lake Valley. Upon arrival, he indicated that prosperity would be his followers' real challenge. Why is it that "a rich man shall hardly enter into the kingdom of heaven" (Matthew 19:23)?

Contentment and security are not as much about adding to riches as subtracting from our desires.

We worry too much about how we look, what we lack, circumstances we cannot change, and what we "should" be.

Contentment is not some destination or accumulation, but a way of living.

I have heard it said that the person with the most toys when he dies wins. Not so. In fact, it's just the opposite.

I use the motto "Hearses don't have luggage racks." Too many unnecessary things clutter and complicate our lives. Be like the wise clergyman who sewed the pockets of his preaching clothes shut to remind him he could take "no thing" with him.

Jesus Christ taught, "A man's life consisteth not in the abundance of things which he possesseth. . . . The ground of a certain man brought forth plentifully: And he thought within himself, saying, what shall I do, because I have no room where to bestow my fruits? And he said, This will I do: I will pull down my barns, and build greater; and there will I bestow all my fruits and my goods. And I will say to my soul, Soul, thou hast much goods laid up for many years; take thine ease, eat, drink, and be merry. But God said unto him, Thou fool, this night thy soul shall be required of thee" (Luke 12:15–20).

Things require maintenance, and maintenance requires time—time that could be spent on people. Don't get me wrong. A toy can help provide a valuable experience. Our family boated. But cutting down on owning toys brings added contentment—think about renting instead. Consider letting someone else assume depreciation and do the storage and maintenance.

It seems the American dream of the late nineteen hundreds has been multiple incomes, multiple cars, and multiple houses. In our new millennium, the American dream deserves a shift in consideration away from the busy, cluttered life to a simple slowing down to refuel, and downsize.

Remember Christmas mornings when the cardboard boxes held more fascination for small children than the newest electronic toy?

Recently, I phoned a long-time friend at the local hardware store who got me an old fridge box. My seventeen-year-old daughter, my first grandson's mom, and I carefully cut and painted windows and doors and then presented our grandson with his favorite gift on Christmas Day. The monetary cost was one roll of packing tape and some paint. Strange thing is, we all wanted one too!

Some of your things might be your enemy if they are expensive, debt inducing, seasonal, require insurance, or depreciate annually. We are told these things will give us added freedom. It's great when they do.

There is certainly nothing wrong with a motor home, a cottage at the lake, a time-share, an expensive toy, or a hobby if you can afford it, it doesn't force you to work more, and it gives you more time with those who matter most.

A few years ago, Karen and I almost bought a vacation package that was supposed to liberate us. Truth is, it would have taken away our ability to plan our own unique trip each year, and now with failing health it would have become a burden. Do not be fooled. We lose freedom when we buy into too many toys, time-shares, and such.

Clutter may also be your enemy. No one will want your clutter when you are gone, so begin decluttering now. We learned to just take a picture of memorabilia. We downsize to a photo and then chuck stuff. The memory remains without the things that clutter.

I love pruning trees. First, I properly remove all dead wood, which weighs them down. Next, I eliminate all crossing branches and ensure all is headed skyward. Likewise, we need to properly cut out busyness, recognize counterproductive praise, and reduce the negative influences of things that conflict with our lasting purpose, lifting others and ourselves upward.

When it comes to money, truly balanced, contented people prune regularly and give some away. In the Church, people willingly give 10 percent of their income, and they are blessed for so doing. For giving to needy, "he [the Lord] doth immediately bless you; . . . and ye are still indebted to him" (Mosiah 2:24).

Your immediate blessing is the lack of selfishness, which so often impedes lasting relationships.

My dad was the most contented man I know. He often spoke of what he called "the big three causes of unhappiness." Dad said most of the world's problems came from misuse of power, sex, or money (often the result of misdirected busyness, believing false flattery, and unwise money decisions). He was right.

Dad had money but would intentionally wear his old pinstriped coveralls into the city. He understood there is emptiness in showiness, and true contentment is found in the everyday, simple, and commonplace.

If you aren't extremely careful, money may even create distinctions, which distance you from the common touch and limit your influence for good.

Julis of our world, I like money, but, ironically, if you are not wise, it will not fill, but rather, empty your tank.

Tune-Up Time

If things clutter up your time, you may wish to reflect.

What things can I liquidate to simplify and save time?

(Yes, I know you worked hard for that. This takes nerve.)

In the future, I will consider renting _____.
And I will consider hiring help for _____.

What phrases will help me so I don't forget the enemies?

To who, less fortunate than myself, will I give?

If I have debt, who will I have help me with my plans to eliminate it?

Debt is a great robber of contentment. A wise man of God once said, "Pay thy debt, and live" (2 Kings 4:1–7). We will discuss debt later. It may be one of your major enemies.

You now see more clearly a few of the enemies to the contented life. We've been trying to clean your windshield and refuel.

Knowing and confronting the enemy may have been a bit painful (you may be wondering, "How did I get myself on this road?"), but now your wipers are working and you're filling your tank. If it helps, you're not alone; we all get fooled. These are some truths I would like to have shared with Juli that day in our yoga room.

As she left, I said, "Juli, you're going back into traffic and I hope we helped. I hope it doesn't take a breakdown for you to see clearly that slight alterations will help. When you think about it, never stopping to address our direction in life is kind of air-headish," I said.

Speaking of not thinking, several blondes went into a bar. They cheered "Fifty days! Fifty days!" until the barkeeper finally asked them why fifty days was so significant.

One blonde replied, " 'Cause we just completed a whole puzzle in fifty days, and right on the box it said two to three years."

This is hard work. You may wish to shut down your engine or just idle awhile. It is up to you.

Next, we take the wheel and determine some future objectives. Contented people always start their journeys with their destinations firmly in mind.

Notes
1. Ashli S. Thompson, "Questions and Answers," *Ensign*, December 2005, 63.
2. Ibid., 64.

Chapter Three

Steering Your Vehicle

*Do not be troubled by your troubles.
And yes, you are steering.*

Rodger emailed me this morning. His broken heart is beginning to mend both physically and emotionally. He said, "Until I read your email about the enemies to contentment, I didn't realize my oversights. One thing that really hit home for me was that on our roads are strategically placed individualized bumps and detours, which are needed to help us develop character for our final trip—home."

He continued, "Things do happen for a reason, and it's how we deal with them that makes us into better people." He's got it!

I emailed back and said, "Life goes on, and though life remains hard, you must forge a new future. Do not be troubled by your troubles. Fine metals take intense heat to smelt and purify. You are being given a chance to be refined by your challenges. Let them make you stronger."

Rodger must have agreed, because he responded with, "Yeah, I guess we never strengthen without struggles. But sometimes it would sure be nice to just coast." I agreed.

Trying not to sound too philosophical, I replied, "Sometimes tough stuff just seems to come our way—through little if any fault of our own. And other times we bring trouble on ourselves through our own unwise choices."

I continued with this story:

Two elderly women were out for a drive. After running three consecutive red lights, the passenger said, "Did you realize you just ran three red lights?"

Her friend responded with, "Oh, am I driving?"

Yes, you are steering. To improve your life, you must focus some of your thoughts. Thoughts always precede action. You must concentrate your thoughts on your future purpose. Stop getting stuck in ruts. Let go of past detours.

Big roadblocks in the quest to capture contentment are unfocused, uncontrolled thoughts. By far, the best definition of happiness I have heard is that happy people have a majority of happy thoughts. Honest Abe felt that a person was about as happy as that person decided to be.

Many are so caught up in traffic they never take time to clarify direction. We are so misled and distracted. Slow down and precisely identify the thoughts that hinder your happiness. For what life purpose are you going to live the future? In the past, you have heeded signs randomly placed along your way by others, but no longer. Now, you will direct traffic.

Don't just bump into proper thoughts and purpose now and then. Find and live by your personal purpose until your trip ends. Sounds corny, but your major focus must be on making this world a better place.

I love the scene in the movie *Dead Poets Society* in which a group of students are gazing at a picture of a graduating class from decades before. Their teacher reminds them, "They're not that different from you." The class in the picture is now six feet under. The boys lean toward the picture, and the teacher tells them the now-dead boys are trying to tell them something. That wisdom was, "Carpe diem, seize the day!"

In the context of this chapter, you will seize the day, discover your purpose, and determine your destination. Your tomorrows are up to you!

Starving, deprived of human dignity, and near death, Victor Frankl gave his last crust of bread to his German captor. Victor realized that the human freedom to choose one's own attitude and direction in any given set of stressful circumstances could not be taken away.

Returning to Dr. Frankl, though a prisoner of war, he found contentment in the most deprived circumstances. So can you. He dreamed of his future. What's your excuse? It may well lie simply in your never clearly defining what your destination will be—what you will and won't do in the future. Let's make certain our ladders lean on the correct wall.

I believe people come with a built-in purpose. Most just never take time to clarify their reason for living. What's yours? Where is most of your time spent now? Remember, do not live life for retirement. It may never come.

One thing's for sure, to live a happy, contented life you must live for a purpose that is bigger than just yourself. Purpose involves helping others. Only you can map out how.

Some years ago I made a study of Stephen Covey's *Seven Habits of Highly Successful People*, a book in which people are asked to contemplate writing a mission statement by which to live the rest of their days. Very therapeutic. In hopes it may help someone write their own, I include my statement.

My Personal Mission Statement—August 2002

I only have one lifetime, but if I live right, one is enough. Here is my mission:

I aspire to no great earthly fame or recognition but, rather, will attempt to avoid busyness, the praise of man, and the negative influences of money, thus being able to befriend all.

I will create a life of simple abundance, contentment, and simplicity.

Most important to me will be the search for truth—I will embrace and teach its principles by word and deed wherever I can find it.

Next will always be my best friend, Karen; our children; and our future grandkids.

I will cherish good friends and others and try to help them along the way.

Nature is to be explored, and I will go there often to be near God. Nature always wears the colors of the spirit.

Sports and fitness are lifetime endeavors. I will always try.

I will pursue my work passionately, whatever it is.

These will form the constant core of my life and travels and will breathe life into my daily plans and goals for an adventure well lived—no regrets. At age fifty-five I will never again work for money but will devote my entire existence to a life of study, strengthening faith, and serving the less fortunate.

The essence of my lifetime is captured in the following thoughts:

I will try to win the affection of children, laugh often and much, appreciate beauty, find the best in others, and leave the world a bit better, whether by our children, well-pruned trees, or an improved social condition. If even one life has been easier because I have lived, I have succeeded. Raising children, loving, respecting, and teaching mankind is what I will do.

I plan on being a doer instead of a selfish little person full of complaints, grieving that the world will not make me happy.

I feel my life belongs to the whole community and world, and it is my privilege to do for it whatever I can. I want to be thoroughly used up when I die.

I believe life is not just a sputtering engine, but one eternal round. It is a car that I drive for now, and I want to make it run as well as possible before handing it on to others.

* * *

Don't for a minute imagine that your mission statement must be something spectacular. Most of us are just ordinary people. Understand it is by small and simple things that great things happen—the world is better because of you. Contemplate your purpose.

Has your life been driven by guilt, duty, or what others think? It's time you lived by your own purpose—love-based, people-centered, and self-determined. If you live a contented, meaningful life, you will prune away the less lasting, thus creating time and space for what matters most.

Your mission statement is more than goals—it defines you. Goals change over time. Purpose remains constant and is imbedded within your goals. I strongly suggest you answer the reflective questions below, and then write a simple mission statement for your future.

Tune-Up Time

What are three statements, bigger than yourself, that you will say of yourself?

As we live the contented life, we would do well to ask ourselves the following before acting, "What legacy will I leave loved ones? Who are those I will serve?"

Imagine you have twenty-four hours to live. What would you do and say? With who would you spend these hours?

A Practical Guide to a Contented Life

My Mission Statement

I thought to myself, *I sure hope Rodger and Juli take time to write their purpose.* There was something powerfully fulfilling when I finally got it down on paper. It gave me direction, a point of reference.

I continued by telling Rodger my latest joke.

"I heard one about unwise decisions the other day. An old man was driving down a freeway when his friend called his cell phone and told him to be careful because the news had just reported there was a vehicle on the divided highway traveling against traffic. The old man thanked his friend and then exclaimed, 'There's not just one car; there are hundreds!' "

I continued, "I'm pretty sure the policeman took all things into account and let him off easy. Like most of our wrong turns, our driver didn't get off course on purpose. Everyone misses the occasional road sign. Don't be too hard on yourself for wrong turns in the past. Just get headed in the right direction now."

I want you to take a break before you read more. The reason many books don't transform us is we are in too big a hurry to move on. I want you to ponder what you have committed to and where you are headed.

Chapter Four

Enjoying the Journey

*Enjoy life;
your car is running.*

Juli dropped by this morning. Money is sometimes tight in their home, and she had some news to share.

"I have a job opportunity," were the first words from her mouth.

"Are you sure it's best for all concerned?" I responded. She has young children, and I know how busy a second job forces one to be. Her husband gets a reasonable wage.

"Yep. We should be able to do it. It's just for a few years of night shift, and we think we can cope," Juli said, trying to convince herself.

I thought to myself, *I know money is a must, but something's wrong when money becomes more important than time. Is this the same girl who was overwhelmed by her hectic pace? Is this the girl who was afraid this life was no dress rehearsal? Does being paid make the difference?*

She didn't catch what she was really saying, and she continued, "Yeah, we can get through it."

I do understand the financial rewards, but I couldn't help but ask, "Isn't time doing things you love and having more time with those you care for more important? Don't you remember your frantic feelings in our last chat?"

Just then Karen brought us a snack, so we paused for a moment. Then I said to Juli, "You know, the greatest hunger in the world is not for food and water. The greatest hunger, which so many of us feel even with a full stomach, is a gnawing hunger for time, direction, purpose, and contentment. Will this job give you that? You may decide to take this job, but plan your trip first and make sure you get all you desire of the few days you spend on earth."

In a purposeful, life-focusing list you will now create for yourself, you will list at least fifty purpose-centered goals to accomplish on your trip.

We all put off living and instead of enjoying the journey, we say we'll be happy when . . .

Juli's mind was made up, and we could see it was no use trying to dissuade her. I hope all goes well. But I do think we are sometimes our own worst enemies.

In life I have decided the truly content stay focused on their life purposes and do not allow themselves to become too distracted.

They ponder the question, what do I want? and then have courage and take few detours. There is nothing inherently wrong with taking a job or saying yes, if contentment can accompany you. But is this really what you want?

Solomon said, "Where there is no vision, the people perish" (Proverbs 29:18).

An architect must meticulously plan for construction and then follow those plans, making minor alterations as the project proceeds. Yet, with our most precious building project of all, our lives, we somehow seldom pause to make blueprints.

I once sat and envisioned running marathons, climbing well-known mountain peaks, and visiting famous places, and then something wonderful happened—I did these things. What if I hadn't dreamed?

I wrote relatively effortlessly a list of fifty things I dreamed of coming true in my lifetime and began checking them off one by one. Run a marathon with my spouse, hike in Alaska, retire at fifty-five. These were all bouncing around loose until I captured them on paper. How good this felt!

Imagine my contentment when I was forced from work at age fifty due to this debilitating disease. What regrets I avoided. Sure, I didn't do all fifty things on my list, but what if I had waited for retirement? I now have new, modified dreams. Writing this book is one.

Just get started. Don't wait. Trust me, life passes quickly. I bless the days I spent alone dreaming. Now it's your turn.

Ron was a busy marriage counselor. He was devoted to his patients and took little time for himself or family. He once received a visit from a client who was in the midst of a nasty divorce. What his client said that day changed Ron's life, and it may change yours.

His client had noticed how very tired Ron appeared, so he told his counselor of a motto he had recently adopted—Enjoy life: your car is running. The patient still grieved over his failed marriage and had decided not to remarry. Today, however, he changed his mind. Perhaps it was later than he thought. Perhaps he should try again.

Sleep eluded Ron as he contemplated his life that night. The next morning he asked for two months off. Though he was worried the people at work would be swamped without him, upon his return he realized there were those who hadn't even known he was gone.

He requested his best friend go with him to Jerusalem—a city they had always dreamed of visiting.

His friend said, "I'm too busy. Some other time."

Ron told his friend his newly acquired motto, and these long-time friends spent time together in Jerusalem.

Imagine the mutual gratitude when, upon his return, Ron's friend became ill and soon passed away.

On his deathbed, this dear friend said, "I am so happy, Ron, that we went to Jerusalem together. I thank God we did not wait too long."

For you too, enjoy life now. Your vehicle is running.

My friend Rodger underwent open-heart surgery at age thirty-five. One of my wife's dental hygiene patients yesterday afternoon spoke of her husband's Hodgkin's disease at age thirty-two. And we, often unnecessarily, spend life at "second jobs."

Before my illness advanced to where I couldn't work anymore, a coworker pulled me aside one day and said, "You know, I've been thinking about you and your illness. I've realized that even if you are miraculously healed in ten or twenty years, you'll get something else and be gone anyway." She's right. We are all, from our births, aging and dying. Though we need some cash, time is our most precious commodity.

You know the saying, "Life is short—eat dessert first." Well, it is true. I actually did this at a wedding I recently attended, and it was great. I had dessert twice.

Superb teachers do what is called extending their influence. In my sixth grade classroom, we wrote secret letters to ourselves at the year's end, predicting our futures in detail—bravely including who we would like to marry in our classrooms. We dreamed about our possible futures. We opened these at their ten-year high school reunions. What a hoot.

Soon after my diagnosis, a friend sensing my sober countenance wisely counseled me to remember, "We're in the fun business." I have often failed and taken life too seriously, but this is good advice. Some dreams must be purpose driven, others just for fun.

All people have what I term inborn smarts. Kids may be math, word, music, art, self, people, body, or nature smart, and so forth. Consider what will make life fun and passionate for you, and do it! What are you just naturally good at? What have you always wanted to try? Who needs your time and love?

Public speaking terrifies most people, but when I speak publicly, it excites me. I feel God in me. What does this for you?

Love life. It's meant to be a great adventure, and when well spent there need be no regrets. Smell lilacs in springtime, marvel as gardens grow, and watch birds—now I even appreciate the sparrows.

My father passed on eighteen years ago, and yet some of his words still echo in my mind: "If you do something, do it right the first time."

Get your pencil (not a pen—there's the teacher in me again) and start visualizing your future. Find and capture your passions and people-driven purposes. Life is empty without these.

Though I didn't, I wanted to say, "Juli, are you sure about that second job? I think you would do well to just enjoy life on less and focus on inexpensive, personal dreams and relationships. You know, it's later than you think."

Now, begin your list.

Tune-Up Time

No one can afford not to write these. Try for fifty. Here is a format you might use. I'm including the space for your top ten.

Remember, it is never too late and dreams do not need to be dramatic—just purpose-centered or fun. Do not repeat the past and simply move about aimlessly. You may want to see all your children happily married, paint, run a marathon, climb a peak, or see a country or two. The sky is the limit—maybe sky dive with your best friend. Karen says my craziest is to climb Mt. Sinai—in the dark.

Dream #1: _____

Plan: _____

_____

Anticipated completion date (not too important): _____

Revisions: _____

_____

Dream #2: _____
Plan: _____
_____
Anticipated completion date (not too important): _____
Revisions: _____
_____

Dream #3: _____
Plan: _____
_____
Anticipated completion date (not too important): _____
Revisions: _____
_____

Dream #4: _____
Plan: _____
_____
Anticipated completion date (not too important): _____
Revisions: _____
_____

Dream #5: _____
Plan: _____
_____
Anticipated completion date (not too important): _____
Revisions: _____
_____

Dream #6: _____
Plan: _____
_____
Anticipated completion date (not too important): _____
Revisions: _____
_____

Dream #7: _____
Plan: _____
_____
Anticipated completion date (not too important): _____
Revisions: _____
_____

Dream #8: _____
Plan: _____
_____
Anticipated completion date (not too important): _____
Revisions: _____
_____

Dream #9: _____
Plan: _____
_____
Anticipated completion date (not too important): _____
Revisions: _____
_____

Dream #10: _____
Plan: _____
_____
Anticipated completion date (not too important): _____
Revisions: _____
_____

On your own, and over time, keep going. Sometimes we do lean our ladders against the wrong wall. We place our energies in non-thoughtful places.

Did you hear the one about why Pilgrims' pants always fall down? It's because they wear their buckles on their hats.

Misplaced efforts can be journey hindering. Now, please take a brisk walk to extend your dreams and heighten your determination to make these a reality.

Chapter Five

Listening for Engine Trouble

Life without inner-self rituals will continue leaving you feeling like you are full of sawdust, a phony, an actor, running on empty.

Rodger had mended from open-heart surgery to the point he could visit again. I was most interested in how his other broken heart was doing since I sent him the chapters you have just read. I wondered if he had written and found any new direction.

"So," I began, "may I see your scars?" He unbuttoned his plaid cowboy shirt and showed me his staples. "Isn't it a great era in which we live, when medicine can do this for us?" I replied. "Guess you're a member of the zipper club now."

He laughed and replied, "Yeah, I sure wish they could operate to fix the heartfelt pain of divorce."

"Some pains can only be fixed by ourselves," I said. "Tell me, did you do some journal writing and make some course corrections for your future?"

"I tried," Rodger replied, "but I had trouble knowing exactly where I wanted to go."

"That's normal. It takes time and mental effort. Just keep driving," I said, and I proceeded to tell him some of the following.

Sometimes in life our challenges seem to come without warning. For example, I once had an uncle speak at a fireside about loving our neighbor. In the middle of that very night my uncle died—at the hands of his next-door neighbor and pretty much without warning. But most often we have some warning before troubles strike.

The most common roadkill in these parts is deer. Our son, Matt, was driving late at night a while ago. Something told him to slow down. He listened to the Spirit and avoided a potentially fatal accident.

In Matt's words, "If I'd been listening to the radio I might not have heard." I was reminded of the words, "The still small voice . . . whispereth through" (D&C 85:6).

Some call this their conscience. Let's not forget that "the Spirit of Christ is given to every man" (Moroni 7:16).

My unseen voice once said to write down every funny thing I heard our five kids say. We're glad we listened. The Giggle Book is still one of the best things Karen and I have ever done.

The truth is, "the kingdom of God is within you" (Luke 17:21).

In our culture, a major enemy to a safer, more contented life is that we listen to the wrong voices and not our own. We listen to the media, music, our cell phone, and our culture instead of being still and listening within.

Too often we let cultural traffic and smog prevent our inner selves from speaking, and our vision is obscured.

Pathways to contentment are inside of you. The fact is, if we cannot find contentment within ourselves, there is little use looking elsewhere.

Sleeping under an open sky and trying to count the stars helps me stay in touch with my inner self. What does this for you?

Our family once hosted a Japanese exchange student from Osaka. We will never forget his wonder as he stood in our driveway late on his first Canadian night and, for the first time in his fifteen years, witnessed the wonder of the stars. He simply stood and sighed. Osaka's many lights had thus far blocked his view—but the stars were there all along.

If you don't know how to get in touch, remember that nature is a key to inner self. Nature always wears the colors of the spirit. Go there to get in touch. We don't need the Hubble telescope to experience wonder.

The best psychiatrist will simply help you uncover your own answers. You just haven't been listening. You've been largely ignoring your own built-in GPS.

Sometimes we hear or read something and we come across an idea that rings a bell. We recognize it to be true, and it just feels right.

We inherited this inner voice from heavenly parents. All of us did. I like to think of this inner voice as God-given headlights to help His children stay on the road.

A friend of ours, long crippled by polio, recently told Karen and me that our difficulties would make us real. We thought we were sincere and genuine before, but she was right. If allowed, difficulty intensifies your inner voice, making you more purposeful, sensitive, genuine, and real.

When we learn to listen for engine troubles, we can avoid breakdowns along our way and keep moving when they do occur.

When our inner self is both heard and obeyed, life becomes an adventure worth living. All problems become solvable.

I said, "Rodger, the answers are within yourself. You came with a Jiminy Cricket, so to speak. Trouble is, Pinocchio often ignores his potential best friend. Ignoring this voice is often what results in our troubles in the first place."

Following this voice in your future, you will be able to distinguish the relevant from the irrelevant, the nice from the necessary, and the busy from the essential. Trials and the subsequent strengthening of this inner voice may help you become real, like Pinocchio did when he listened.

As a young university student, I tried sciences, then the arts. Finally I listened to an emotion that said, "Teach." The mind said, "They don't pay teachers enough," but the heart said, "Teaching leads to contentment (and summers off)," and the inner voice was right again.

My brother was accepted into dental school. He has a brilliant mind, yet, though accepted, he voluntarily opted out. Wade listened to his heart and went to Harvard instead to become a city planner.

In my opinion, you may not be listening carefully enough (your engine may be knocking) if you live under the weight of any of the following enemies of contentment—undue debt, not spending quiet time with "hand of God" books (more about these later), gossiping, thinking you are somehow defective or better than others, being driven by guilt, constantly feeling hurried, trying to rescue others from the natural consequences of their actions, ridiculing those whose position deserves our respect, refusing to forgive, or worrying excessively. Debt is of particular concern.

These are just a few engine lights to watch for to help avoid an inevitable breakdown or becoming stuck. Listen to the inner self and let it direct you.

Being untrue in marriage likely breaks up more potentially content relationships than any other single cause, and reckless spending of money you have not yet earned is right behind infidelity. Money mismanagement causes unwanted stress, a lack of peace of mind, and is an unwelcome bedfellow in healthy, contented relationships. Do not ignore your debts but instead reach out for roadside assistance if necessary.

Getting in touch with your inner voice can be achieved in a variety of ways—running, climbing mountains, walking, focused meditation, journaling, yoga, prayer, fasting, being alone in nature, listening to inspirational music, encouraging others, reading, etc. Discover what works for you. Now set aside a time to practice it regularly (you need and deserve it).

Slow down. Make it a ritual. Life without inner-self rituals will continue leaving you feeling like you are full of sawdust, a phony, an actor, running on empty.

I don't know about you, but if I limit myself to my own mundane thoughts, I risk becoming terribly bored. Include meaningful reading in your lifelong inner-self rituals, and you will hear this voice more clearly.

I live in North America, a land of peace and unusual prosperity, yet I am concerned that even North Americans forget to count their blessings. We become disgruntled over trivialities like the temperature of a beverage, traffic, or slow service at a drive-thru. How much more content we are when we stop and consider our gifts. Do not go down the ungrateful road.

A friend says this world can be like an onion—it is round, it stinks, and it is going to make you cry. Though our world can be this way, we need to maintain an attitude of gratitude. Be like the elderly woman who looks in the mirror one morning and sees she is losing her hair. With just three hairs left, she decides she'll braid them and has a great day. With two hairs, she decides she'll part down the middle, and with one she decides it's time for a ponytail. With no hair left, she exclaims, "Yes! I don't have to do my hair today." Now that's the way to think.

Selfishness may also be a major barrier to heeding the inner voice. You might not be listening if you say "I" and not "we," or "mine" and not "ours." Do not show your ignorance of others' feelings and importance to you by your choice of words. They say that light travels faster than sound, and so I believe that some people appear bright until they speak.

For years, one of my rituals included a gratitude journal in which I wrote three things that were working reasonably well in my life every day. Wise is the person who does not take time to number all his troubles. Sometimes I list how my life could be worse. Trust me, you do not have to look far to see someone with who you would not trade.

I believe that ignoring your inner voice is like ignoring a low tire. Eventually, you will be forced to stop. Much better to listen, stop, and address the problem before being stranded.

Life has challenges. Don't ignore your inner voice and thereby create challenges through hurtful, careless choices. God can do all repairs, but listening to your inner voice reduces your unnecessary pains.

You are one of this universe's miracle creations. There is a spark of indefinable divinity and goodness in each of you. Take time and get in touch with the real you. Find your voice, then obey.

You may have been too busy to listen in the past, but no more. If all you see and hear in life comes through your eyes and ears, you don't learn much about living. Learn to follow feelings—listen and obey your heart.

Think of a time you withstood reason and followed your inner prompting. (Makes you smile, doesn't it?)

You may wish to grab your pencil. Remember, real happiness (listening to inner voice) is seldom done in crowds. It is found in quiet. It is most often found in solitude and reflection.

Tune-Up Time

What engine troubles are you experiencing by ignoring your inner voice? Listen. (Go back and see if any of the ones we discussed in this chapter sound familiar.)

What will you do about each issue?

What will your rituals be? Maybe you already have some. When will you do them?

Does your speech prove you guilty of being selfish? What words will you change?

* * *

"Rodger," I said, "from here on out, you must stay in closer touch with the real you."

"I will try," was his response. "No more aimlessly following other voices."

Rodger was working twelve plus hours a day—that's half of his life.

"Hey, I heard a good joke you'd enjoy," I said. "A man mistreats his wife for years. Then she dies. Saint Peter tells her that to enter heaven she must spell a word. The word is *love*. She easily spells it correctly and then happily enters. Years pass, and so does her husband. She asks Saint Peter if she can welcome him in, and he appropriately permits. She meets her husband at the pearly gates and tells him he simply needs to spell a word to enter. He says, 'So, what's the word?' and she replies, '*Czechoslovakia.*'"

Take an hour or two off. Practice your rituals if possible. See if they are right for you.

Chapter Six

Avoiding Dead Ends

*Our view of reality
is our reality.*

Juli was a bit stressed today because she said no to friends who wanted her to babysit for a week while they vacationed in Aruba.

"Juli, why does this have you so upset?" I asked, knowing her answer before she gave it.

"Because she's my friend, and I should help her," she replied. Juli lives the guilt-driven life. Some say all women do. Juli was living under the weight of a crushing false belief. She actually believed that it was somehow her responsibility to rescue her friend. She had the disease to please.

Happiness stems from a way of thinking of life.

"Juli, a while back I promised myself never to use the word *should*. It is guilt-ridden. During those growing up years, we have all accumulated a few of what I call false beliefs—words we use and lies we live. Let me show you how to address these."

A few years ago my principal noticed I was tense and stressed, so he invited me to sit at the feet of a much older woman and see if she could help. I was skeptical to say the least. I could be "getting something done" instead of wasting my time. I was so wrong.

I had always considered Aunt Bea unique. A former teacher herself, I was always happy I had escaped her tutelage. She was the teacher who fed brown bread to one rat and white to another to show kids the effects of good nutrition. She fed kids dandelion leaf salad, made rose-hip tea, and had you do headstands on the school's two-story balcony to rid you of headaches. Now a teacher myself, I was to be her reluctant pupil after all.

I discovered this woman to be deeply compassionate and insightful over the coming years. She taught me that feelings are the direct result of thoughts, and if my thoughts were untrue, I would remain fretful, full of fear, and unfulfilled. Surprise! She was right. It was how I thought and what I said that determined my feelings.

Let me illustrate. In high school I was number thirteen and point guard on the basketball team. This unlucky jersey number embarrassed me. Until one day I changed my thoughts and told an opponent he was right, it was unlucky—for his team. I requested this jersey in the future. How I thought and spoke made all the difference.

Each of us has different experiences that have shaped our present. But we can also change our way of thinking.

From the realization that thoughts govern emotion, I felt freed. First, I would identify personal, stress-inducing false beliefs formed out of my past, and then I would begin replacing them with the truth. You wouldn't believe my increased gas mileage.

Soon I will give you three personal examples of my false beliefs to help illustrate—realizing that your own false beliefs may be very different.

A contented life is a life of self-examination and course corrections. Your mind can be either a prison or a palace. The choice is yours.

The way we interpret our experiences sometimes teaches lies we accept and buy into. We must reach a place where we no longer think, speak, or act on such falsehoods.

For example, abused children who are told they are stupid are truthfully not this way—they are, in fact, smart but under-appreciated. It's a big lie they are told.

We must learn to assume responsibility for ourselves and reject the subtle lies we are told.

For future contentment, you must limit wrong turns, identify lies you're living, and revise them. We all live out some untruths.

In this chapter I ask you to think about your thinking.

I am very competitive. My father taught me, "Why play a game if you aren't there to win?" This served me well for many years in competitive sports, but then I married and had children. When playing with them, my old belief did not serve me well.

I thought of a beloved grandma. I am convinced she let her grandchildren win in Rook whenever we played her.

Our view of reality is our reality. If our road map is false and inaccurate, we'd do well to make the effort and alter our maps. This rewriting the script requires effort. The process of revising is painful, and so we avoid confronting the lies with which we are familiar. Just as a rocket exerts most energy at lift-off, a person must exert the most energy while overcoming the pull of the past, but the process becomes easier with time.

For years at our school it was falsely believed that students in grades one through three must enter a separate door from those in grades four through six. As administrators, we discussed the validity of changing what had become an ingrained tradition, and we decided to change. This simplified life for all concerned.

You might think you can't change, but a wise principal reminded me that sometimes long-cherished false beliefs need addressing.

Your most trip-hindering thoughts may include comparing yourself to someone else. Never do this. Compare yourself only with the yesterday you.

From the epiphany of Aunt Bea's sessions regarding the power of my thoughts over my general sense of well being, my life has included times spent identifying personal false beliefs and then replacing them with the truth.

Here are three examples. I will illustrate each with a personal story.

False Belief #1—No one can do my job as well as I can, and someday I will be greatly missed.

Truth: Though good at what I do, I am easily replaced most everywhere, and usually only a precious few will really even notice I'm gone.

I worked for twenty-five years at one school. For a time, I actually believed I was irreplaceable. Good thing I learned otherwise. Now the day came when I would leave—surprise!—on disability. As needs be, I had worked hard, caring deeply about my work.

True, no one will do the job exactly the way I did, but, nonetheless, my presence was not necessary to the running of an effective school.

Sometime when you are feeling important, your ego is bursting, or you feel you are outstanding, remember that most of what you do is like the hole left in a bucket of water when you remove your hand.

Care passionately about the people you serve at work, but sometime when you feel your going would leave an unfillable hole, realize this is one of the lies many live.

False Belief #2—I must choose a career based on what my parents expect and then become wealthy.

Truth: Parents simply want us to be content.

I was busy living out a lie. I ended up where I belonged, but it took effort to change this false belief.

Funny how we create our own limitations sometimes. Both my brother and I lived under the false belief that our parents expected us to be wealthy. As before mentioned, Wade was actually accepted into dental school and I spent time on a similar road.

False Belief #3—We somehow owe our children a college education.

Truth: We owe our children teachings, love, support, and encouragement. The rest is up to them.

Friends of mine, like so many parents I know, lived under the power of this false belief. You even see financial institutions on TV trying to get you to "buy in." My friends worked extra years at an advanced age in failing health, even going in debt to pay for their children's education. This is admirable but certainly unnecessary. Do you believe this financial institution really had this couple's best interest in mind?

Children learn much by meeting their own needs while parents need simply lend a hand where possible. Only in this generation, with our current prosperity, do we invent such stress-inducing false beliefs.

We produce much of our own stress by living out false beliefs. Spend time identifying and rewriting your own road map.

Tune-Up Time

List your top three stress-inducing, energy-consuming false beliefs, and replace them with the truth. Try it. Listen to the voice inside. Fill your tank and conserve fuel. Limit dead ends. Do not skip this.

False Belief #1: _____
Truth: _____
_____
_____
_____

False Belief #2: _____
Truth: _____
_____
_____
_____

False Belief #3: _____
Truth: _____
_____
_____
_____

* * *

"Juli, are you still going to feel guilty for saying no?" I asked.

Realizing she was partly still living under the cloud of her own false belief, she wisely answered, "You know I never thought this way before, but I have my own family to care for. I'm not responsible for my friend's vacation. My husband and I share such little time alone as it is. My friend is my friend—not my responsibility. I'm glad I said no."

I wanted to shout, "Yes!" but didn't.

A question to ask yourself when someone asks you to share figurative gas is, "Do I have a stewardship or responsibility over this?" If not, you have every right (maybe even the responsibility) to say no. Remember the ten virgins who were asked to share their oil? They didn't rescue, they said no (Matthew 25:1–13).

"Sometimes we cause our own chaos by the way we perceive experiences. Hey, that reminds me of a good one about chaos. Have you got time for a joke?" I asked.

We have a great lawyer friend who takes us to rock concerts, so I can tell this next joke.

A doctor, engineer, and lawyer were all arguing about which profession was the most important. The doc claimed God was a surgeon because He had taken from Adam a rib. In his defense, the engineer used the Creation and reminded us that before the Creation there was nothing but chaos. The lawyer responded with, "And who do you think makes chaos?"

* * *

Instead of babysitting her friend's kids, Juli spent some long-overdue time with her own loved ones and felt somewhat refueled.

Chapter Seven

Accidents Happen

Forgiveness is an act of self-love.
Forgive or perish.

Rodger called to tell me he had found some inner-self rituals that seemed to be helping. He said he was walking alone, spending more time in prayer, and enjoying some great books for the first time in years. He's still not well, so we email.

In one of Rodger's emails he said, "My one big challenge is to pray for my wife . . . My bitterness is overpowering." True, it is hard. Forgiveness is one of the most difficult virtues to develop. Forgiveness is indeed God-like.

Yet God says that to ever be completely content, you must be able to "pray for them which despitefully use you, and persecute you" (Matthew 5:44). God ought to know. He has plenty of people to forgive.

I responded to Rodger's email. "All of us make mistakes and need Father's forgiveness. Do you think Father will forgive us when we refuse to forgive His other children? I don't."

The Lord says, "I . . . will forgive whom I will forgive, but of you it is required to forgive all men . . . ye ought to say in your heart . . . let God judge between me and thee" (D&C 64:10–11).

"I don't want to offend you, Rodger, but I believe that unless you forgive, the greater burden is yours. An offense is only an offense if taken. Which is better, to suffer an injustice or to commit one?"

If I could have continued writing, I'd have told him a story.

There are days and pains we never forget. I recall the day my cousin and I accidentally burned down our neighbor's barn. We tried running to the local swimming pool, hoping our problem would just go away. Soon we heard the sirens and were called home.

The very next day was even more memorable, as Mom marched me across the alley to apologize to Mrs. Blaxall. What a long walk. But it was worthwhile. It was like getting a luggage rack off my shoulder. This lesson still serves me well.

I don't care what your faith, color, or culture may be. Happiness is found in simple goodness and a clear conscience.

Sometimes as we drive, we do dumb things. There are tickets, fender benders, and even fatal accidents. I have witnessed a great tragedy in life, even within my faith. Most people limit what they believe their Heavenly Father is willing to repair for them. They somehow believe that what they have done or not done is just too much. What gives anyone the right to limit God?

A dear church friend of mine had made the decision to forgive a spousal affair and stay with her husband. She was trying desperately to make things work. A second church-attending woman met her on the street and wrongfully said, "You weak woman. Haven't you left him yet?"

My forgiving friend is one of my heroes to this day. I feel sorrow for the second woman's bitterness. God cares less about what we have or have not done and more about what we do with our futures. Forgive yourself, then all others.

Ignore this and you allow others to steer your vehicle, and your contentment remains in park. "See that you do not judge wrongfully; for with that same judgment which ye judge ye shall be judged" (Moroni 7:18). Judge someone's driving? Maybe. But never judge the driver.

My favorite story to illustrate our need to forgive is about a young boy who sat atop a mountain. There appeared to him a rattlesnake beckoning to be carried to the warmer plain below. The snake promised he would not harm the boy. So the boy reluctantly picked up the cold, docile serpent.

When they reached the prairie below, the rattler struck, injecting the boy with deadly venom. The boy's first thought was, *How could you do this after all I have done for you?* He dropped the uncaring snake, which slithered into a nearby bush.

His first impulse was to pick up a stick and angrily chase after the snake so as to get even. Instead, he chose to seek help. The boy had a crucial decision to make for his future. *Do I seek an antidote or revenge?*

In the contented life, forgiveness and seeking to understand are the antidote when we have been crashed into. Never forget that forgiveness is an act of self-love. Forgive or perish.

Yes, you may remember your pain so as not to pick up rattlers again, but you don't have to carry your venom around, poisoning yourself and everyone else.

To me, the Bible story of Joseph being sold into Egypt epitomizes the principle of forgiveness. After being threatened, abused, and then sold as a slave, he forgave his would-be murderous brothers and prospered. Instead of returning hurt for hurt, he frankly forgave them and later saved their lives and his own (Genesis 37–45).

Rodger, if you are ever to capture contentment, you must arrive at forgiveness, and it can be a very long journey. Get on your way. Begin by asking God's forgiveness yourself. Then pray for enemies. Otherwise, you'll continue running on fumes.

Once you've offered sincere apologies, do not repeat them. They're history.

Tune-Up Time

This maintenance is perhaps the most crucial in keeping you running smoothly. Forgiving is like unhitching a heavy burden you've been towing around, draining your fuel. Get a pencil and then consider the following.

Do you need to get started by saying, "I'm sorry" or "I'm trying to forgive"? Who to?

What do you need to say? Can't say it in person just yet? Perhaps writing and sending these thoughts is a place to begin.

What would you like to be able to say and mean? (No excusing yourself now.) Someday you will be able to mean it.

What will you think to help you forgive?

* * *

I hope you can eventually forgive. It is not only nice, but it's essential for your future contentment. It may take years to achieve, but you can get there. There is a peaceful life awaiting you, and this too will pass away if you so choose. I know—I've seen it.

"Saying sorry and meaning it is serious stuff, but it's essential. Now, let's laugh," I insisted.

My family is made up of at least three generations of Yankee baseball fans. You either love the Yanks or you hate 'em. Many friends dislike the Yanks, but I personally do not apologize for my admiration. Instead, I tell this joke. What is the difference between a Yankee Stadium hotdog and a Fenway Park (home of the Boston Red Sox, the Yankees' arch rival) hotdog? The answer is, you can still buy a Yankee hotdog in October (during the World Series).

Rodger, contentment is waiting for you to reach out and claim it. Even when uncalled for, apologize, say, "I'm so sorry," and mean it. I know it helps hearts heal.

Chapter Eight

No Worries

*Worrying will not liberate you from tomorrow's sorrows;
it will only empty you of today's gasoline.*

Don't for one minute think that every time Juli visits it is to discuss her problems. We have happy visits too. But today the world again presented her with a tank-emptying concern.

"I'm worried sick," Juli said, sitting herself down on our small, comfortable sofa.

"What's wrong?" I asked, hoping it wasn't too serious.

"I can't pinpoint it," she said. "I just worry all the time, and I am so tired of it."

I wanted to go right to, "Juli, worrying will not liberate you from tomorrow's sorrows. It will only empty you of today's gasoline," but I knew that, though true, it would sound too pat and preachy.

Juli's enemy was worry itself.

A wise mother counseled her son, "About the present shed few tears, and about the future harbor no fears."

A mentor of mine was once asked why he was successful. He responded, "I take no counsel from my fears."

They say the number one fear in America is public speaking and number two is dying. Does this mean we'd rather be in the casket than at the pulpit?

I told Juli about a friend of mine who had recently loaded her young children into the mini-van and headed out alone on a long trip. Her engine started overheating, and she feared the worst. Having worried herself sick the entire trip, she arrived safely, only to discover there was no major problem. There was simply some long prairie grass plugging her radiator. Her tiring hours of worry had proven needlessly draining.

On our honeymoon we almost starved because a "friend" had hot-wired our horn to the lights. We worried and thought we couldn't go out after dark for fear of disturbing the peace. Had I looked closer, I'd have seen that simply removing a strategically placed extra wire could have solved the dilemma. Worry causes unnecessary breakdowns and seldom is as serious as we imagine.

Do not look forward to this life in fear; for as troubles arise, God, whose you are, will deliver you out of them, or He will shield you and give you faith to carry your burdens.

I love that Aussies say, "No worries." They've got it right. Worrying is fruitless.

We could have worried ourselves sick when our oldest son got some friends together, bought a one-dollar car, and headed to Vegas, but what good would it have done?

My father was an eighteen-year-old soldier in WWII. Upon his return he told me he never feared anything again. He had been liberated.

No matter what your beliefs, a universal truth is, the contented soul lives by faith—not fear. In fact, fear and faith cannot exist in the same mind.

In any setting along your road, the essential ingredient to contentment and beating fear is trust in God. Happiness has much to do with a refusal to fear.

Many people's greatest worry is what others think of them. Some people fear being fired, others fear rejection. Whatever your fear—stop. Instead, do something about it.

If you worry about what others think about you, wake up and realize they don't. If you can't enjoy your work then consider changing. If you fear rejection, then discuss this with those concerned. Laying fears and concerns on the table is essential and, though a bit frightening, in the end rids you of prolonged, gas-guzzling anxiety.

Your chosen work needs to become a source of contentment and so often is not. I'm not suggesting you run out and tender your resignation. Change or at least stop complaining, and instead think, *How can I make someone else happy at work today?* You cannot help fill others' tanks without getting a few fumes on yourself.

The truth is, you are a competent, appreciable, capable person, able to begin acting instead of feigning helplessness. You choose fear over faith in yourself and your future. Contented people may even have the attitude of "Bring on the rain!"

Sometimes well-meaning people can invite needless worry. A few years ago a young mother and her infant died in a shocking accident. Our community mourned. Some worried for the infant because she lacked a Christian baptism. This is not the God I worship. He said, "I love little children with a perfect love; and they are all alike and partakers of salvation" (Moroni 8:17).

With God there is no value in worry except the worry that causes you to make course corrections.

A friend of mine was being told he must be baptized into a certain faith, even without believing, or be condemned to hell. He worried and asked what I thought. I told him I did not believe in a hell in the traditional sense and not to worry. Because of God's immense love and compassion for us, if we seek the truth and labor with all of our hearts, we will end up in a place of great glory (D&C 76).

I believe Father even reaches out to those who never knew Him while here in life (D&C 138).

Don't worry about getting fairness in the next life. You have heard that life's not fair, right? I interpret this saying differently. We don't deserve the goodness we will receive—that's why life's not fair. We'll receive maximum mercy. Father loves us all.

Many faiths would have you fear and worry about death and meeting God. In scripture, whenever you read, "Fear God" simply replace the word *fear* with *respect* or *reverence*. You do not fear someone who loves you and who you can trust completely.

It is obvious to any careful observer of life that God loves differences. People come in all shapes, sizes, colors, beliefs, and cultures. There are some things about ourselves we cannot change, but fearing is not one of them.

Contented people—those who understand God and know where they are traveling—do not worry; instead they trust. God is love. "There is no fear in love" (1 John 4:18).

Tune-Up Time

You may find it useful to put your fears down on paper. Consider the following.

What is your greatest worry?

Try to articulate why this is a worry.

What will you think to help drive out this worry?

* * *

Your worries are often rooted in your own self-created, false beliefs. Flip back to the chapter titled "Avoid Dead Ends" and replace your major worry with the truth you have just bumped into.

Juli, let me close with a joke about a man who had a problem but did not fear. He stared challenge in the eye and got what he wanted out of life.

A guy goes into a bar and says, "Give me a drink before the trouble starts." He does this repeatedly until the barkeeper finally asks, "So when is this trouble going to start?" The man responds with, "When I tell you that I don't have any money."

So, Juli, I know it is easy to find something to worry about—to give in to fears—but remember, fear and faith do not exist in the same heart. Identify and drive out your fears. You can and must do this.

Chapter Nine

Traveling My Way

*Use the KISS principle—Keep It Simple, Stupid.
Also, learn to think outside the box.*

From the moment I awake, my days seem to go downhill, as far as my body goes, so one day I was just sitting and, out of frustration, feeling a bit sorry for myself. I was thinking, *Why is my vehicle broken when the driver inside still wants so badly to go to the dance?* Just then I was rescued by a knock on the back door as it opened.

"Hi, Rodger," I said, struggling to stand. "How goes it today?" I paused while he sat. Then I continued quite directly, "I hope you have some happy news for me. Have you been able to begin forgiving?"

"I'm making progress," was his reply. "I need time."

"Yeah, I imagine. It is not easy changing the way we respond to pain," I said. "But remember, it is worth it. Forgiveness is an act of self-love, and there is so much good a forgiving person can do in the future."

"Yeah, I guess I have to look at things differently. There is my old life, and now my new life," he said, looking down at the floor.

Trying to cheer him, I said, "It's true, Rodger, no use worrying about gas you've already burned or milk you've spilled. Just refuel, clean it up as best you can, then stay focused on future contentment. There is still plenty of fun and purpose out there. By the way, did you hear the one about the creative, quick-thinking speeder?"

"No," was his answer. So I told him.

"A cop pulls a guy over for going too fast and asks to see his driver's license. The driver explains he has ten DUIs and lost his license. He then said his registration is in his glove box beside his pistol, and his girlfriend's dead body is in his trunk. The officer radios backup, and when help arrives the second policeman asks the driver for his license, which is promptly produced. The backup officer then checks the glove compartment and trunk, where he finds nothing. When questioned about the first officer's claims, the driver responds, 'Oh, that liar probably told you I was speeding too.'"

All too often people readily believe what others say and think of them. This can lead to serious misreadings in life.

My father was the epitome of traveling his own way—of not caring what people thought. His wearing pinstriped work coveralls to the city used to embarrass me so much. Now I rather admire his attitude. He had learned to be content with modest means, to seek comfort over fashion, and he emphasized character above others' opinions. He would visit endlessly, hurry never, and he cherished the company of children and ditchdiggers as much as kings. Dad showed me that happiness is largely found in the common.

An old Frank Sinatra tune looks back on a life with no regrets and says, "I did it my way."

This does not mean you just do what you want with no regard for consequences. The ten "traffic laws" given on Mt. Sinai (see Exodus 20) help us avoid accidents and still point us toward lasting contentment.

Yet, all too often, people march to a rhythm played by someone else. It's kind of like the difference between letting the radio play randomly and selecting your own music.

In the last few chapters, you have begun composing your own tune—charting a new course. Here I will present three more tips to help you keep driving on full.

First, in teaching and in life, success largely depends on our ability to condense or simplify. Some call this the KISS Principle—Keep It Simple, Stupid.

I was repulsed by the teacher jargon used to confuse or leave certain people entirely blank on a subject. Instead, try to simplify all you do and say. It was my goal to keep life in the classroom and elsewhere simple.

It is helpful to understand the process of condensation. It is essential to know it is wet when it rains. Forgetting this KISS principle gets in the way of contentment. Can you somehow simplify your life? How?

This would be my simplified lesson on various potentially complex issues:

Government—Vote, disagree if you want, and get along.
Religion—Love one another, even the differences.
Nature—Explore, enjoy, and reverence.

Try to travel lighter and get at the core of things.

Another practice content people must nurture is the idea of creative fun, even silliness. I used to encourage my sixth graders to solve their own problems creatively. One day in art, Danny, a student of mine, complained he'd left his paintbrush at home and asked if he could use mine. He could see no other solution.

My response was, "You can solve this problem. Think outside the box." And he did. I watched him remove the small eraser from his pencil, clip a bright red lock of his own hair (thank goodness he used his own), then tape and glue it all together. His work was completed on time. I would never have thought of that. The lesson Danny taught me that day was that we could sometimes avoid problems and find success by not simply following the crowd—by thinking outside the box. Life is meant to have an element of fun and creativity.

Once, while compiling report card marks, I found myself musing over the fact that what the children were most concerned about was their artwork completion. Like a typical adult, I thought to myself, *What about the really important curricular material like math, science, and social studies?* The kids were teaching me again.

Soon after Danny's experience, at my wife's persuasion I acted outside the box and got silly myself. I recall sending home fake report cards one April Fool's Day. Everything in them was false, including comments I'd never use like "slow learner" and "hopeless." We had a good laugh that day.

What saddened me was how even the top students and their parents believed the worst. Why is it we so readily believe the bad?

We adults take our lives too seriously. Sometimes we even skip art altogether, and it is the fun, silly, creative part we will hold dearest.

Shel Silverstein writes a beautiful parable called *The Giving Tree*. It tells of a tree that loved a boy. This tree gave the boy his all trying to make him happy. At one point, the boy has grown into a man and says he is too busy to climb tree trunks and swing from branches. The grown man has completely forgotten the happy little boy inside.

I have had singular experiences few ever enjoy. Twice, in public, I have been hurled from a wheelchair. Once, forward (you should have seen the onlooker). Then another time I lay prostrate on the asphalt in the parking lot after Karen ran the Salt Lake City Marathon. Now, though I don't wish for a repeat, I actually cherish these memories.

I recall the drive home after seeing the movie *Field of Dreams*. Cruising past the city baseball diamond, I noticed the baseball park with the game lights still on and casually commented to Karen, "I always wanted to play under the lights." She's great. That's all it took.

Karen rented the park, I called twenty old baseball friends (none of who said no), and the game was on. Thank goodness someone reminded me from time to time to be childlike.

In our current circumstances, Karen is teaching me to think outside the box. Dates now include purchasing movies rather than visiting theaters, drive-thrus instead of restaurants, taking long naps, and having friends over instead of going out.

A third sign on the contentment highway involves children. A niece of ours just found out she will never be able to bear children. After sorrowing a brief moment, I thought, *Thinking outside the box, one could view this as an opportunity to raise a diverse family. She could use adoption to raise children from a variety of backgrounds and circumstances.*

I love children. I believe children make life worthwhile. Whether you have your own or not, children enrich lives. I do not know of a school that would not encourage your volunteer involvement with children.

If kids made this world's "big" decisions, I can assure you that there would be no hunger, things would be more fair, our social issues would be addressed rationally, and we'd take more recesses.

Kids help you stay childlike. In today's world many couples entirely miss their ride when it comes to genuine, lasting contentment. I have wonderful friends who will not have children for the sake of a mortgage—and a few hassles.

King David, father of Solomon, who many deem the wisest man to have lived, counseled us to have children. Today, having kids is less common, but don't let culture fool you. David said of kids, "Happy is the man that hath his quiver full of them" (Psalm 127:5).

We have five children, and giving life and love to a child has become the single most meaningful experience of my life.

In my opinion, any mother who has done her best to raise her children deserves a seat in heaven. Surprise! It is in doing the hard things that we find lasting contentment.

Successful marriages and families take sacrifice, but the love and contentment they can produce is real and lasting.

In Chris VanAlsburg's book *The Polar Express*, the adults had forgotten life's magic—they could not hear the Christmas bell. Only a child had ears to hear.

I sometimes think children have their own conception of God, and we'd do well to reverence their God and nurture the little child within us.

When mortality ends, we will wish we had simplified, taken a few more chances, been a bit more artistic and more childlike, been sillier, taken longer recesses, and not been so serious.

On today's highway travel millions who are troubled, uncertain, and confused. They are frustrated because they are lost. They can't see the forest for the trees. They need to lighten up.

It is fundamental that you relax and enjoy yourself. Work and duty are important, but play is essential to a contented life.

Too many adults wear costumes and act out parts they imagine adults are expected to play. I'm convinced God takes time to dance. A great hidden secret is found in the familiar childhood song that ends with the words, "Life is but a game."

As an adult, I sometimes view life as a rusty, beat-up, almost empty car just trying desperately to keep on moving, let alone have some fun. Your vehicle may have been muddied. It's no fault of your own that life's puddles may have tossed dirt on you. You may feel you have no time to simplify, to be silly, or include children—you're wrong. If you live like you've always lived, you will get out of life what you've always gotten.

For the past ten years, each day at school, right after singing "Oh, Canada," I read the entire school the joke for that day.

From now on, no longer eliminate simplicity, silliness, or small children. These will add more contentment to your life.

We all have expected roles we must somewhat play, but that now I am mostly through playing, I ask myself, "What devil possessed me that I conformed to my surroundings so well?"

"Rodger, I would take away your troubles, but they are yours to learn from. Thank you for trusting me enough to talk. As serious as life is, it still needs an element of fun. I hope I haven't offended you—if so, too bad. Just kidding. Hey, have you heard what the blonde said when she looked in the Cheerio box?"

"No," he replied.

"Donut seeds!" I said.

We need to find the fun in life because no one gets out of here alive. Part of my illness results in uncontrollable laughter. Funny thing is the doc wants to medicate me. I think I'll seek out humor instead. Stay awake to fun.

Tune-Up Time

What did you enjoy as a child (for me it was art class) that you have forgotten? Is it on your list of fifty goals?

What will you do to not take yourself so seriously? To reawaken the child in you?

* * *

It was election time and one disgruntled listener jeered that he wouldn't vote for a certain candidate if the politician were Saint Peter himself. The quick-thinking candidate responded that if he were Saint Peter, this voter wouldn't even be in his district.

Have the courage to travel your way.

Chapter Ten

Approaching Marriage

*Paramount among life's decisions
is the choice of who to marry.*

For years I have felt the need for a compulsory, realistic course for all considering marriage. Included would be topics such as finances, spousal needs, and sex.

"Juli, a major source of contentment lies in having a trusting relationship. It is seldom good to be alone."

"I don't know how some people do it," Juli replied.

"Not everyone even gets one chance at a meaningful relationship in this life. How grateful we ought to be," I replied.

"I know, but my marriage could use some nurturing," she said, nodding her head in agreement.

"Whose couldn't?" I replied. The following are my eclectic thoughts on the most sacred subject of marriage.

Paramount among life's decisions is the choice of who to marry. Who will become my best friend—mother or father to my children? With whom will I begin and end each day and night? Who will be beside me on bad hair days, during sickness, and even death?

I preface my remarks boldly that readers may understand somewhat the weight of this monumental decision.

In this earth life, there is no other relationship with such power to heal or to hurt. I have seen many tears shed by spouses and by children over an unhappy, troubled marriage.

For men especially, divorce and the attendant pain can lead them to the psychiatric ward or worse—to the point of losing all desire to live. Only the love of truth, which never lets us down, has the power to rescue them.

One day a young girl brought a large, concealed knife to school. She was just fifteen but overflowing with pain and anger.

"Why did you bring the knife?" I asked.

"I'm running away. Got it all planned. Hitchhiking to Calgary, and if some jerk tries anything, I'll use it on him." Her close male friend had recently taken his own life.

Most poignant were the words she spoke as I tried to help her feel that I understood just a bit of her pain. She replied with, "Well, your parents weren't divorced, were they?" She was the victim of two failed marriages. We sit on the edge of an angry future generation, and many will be the children of divorce. We must do our best to curb this anger.

Now, based on almost thirty years of happy marriage to my best friend and years of counseling couples through their troubled times, I have come to several conclusions regarding just how one can know who this mystery person is and how to love and cherish a spouse so that love and friendship continue to grow. With this knowledge, I hope the pain of divorce might be avoided.

Falling in love, one person reflected, is finding someone just right, someone you love like the best pal you ever had and the worst crush you ever had too.

Finding a person to love is the ultimate treasure hunt. Sometimes it's best to pay more heed to actions, like opening car doors, than you give to their words.

Once you are confident that you have found this wonderful and mysterious individual who treats you well and who you can trust completely, take your decision to Father and then simply listen. Hormones aside, does it feel right?

First and foremost, there must be between you a strong, burning physical attraction. You must like the way he walks and talks. Her smell, her voice, her way of dress, her laughter, and her every movement must be irresistible to you. When your initial courting is complete, and the challenges and day-to-day demands of marriage present themselves, as they inevitably will, you will become aware of small idiosyncrasies you were unaware of during those exciting courtship days.

In our living room there used to hang an invaluable Navajo rug. Its worth was partly due to its imperfections. There were actually burrs woven into this one-of-a-kind rug, thus increasing the rug's value.

People are like this. Viewed properly, our idiosyncrasies (much like the burrs) make each of us the one-of-a-kind person we are and actually increase our uniqueness and worth.

Yes, there are legitimate reasons to divorce, but generally, once married, remember that you have made your choice and now must do all in your power to make your marriage work. It is often uphill, especially raising children together, but it is the greatest of adventures and will lead you toward contentment.

You will make sacred promises with your future spouse. Resolve within yourself to follow this counsel. Instead of trying to get rid of each other, remember that you have made your choice. Strive to honor and keep promises; do not say that you have acted unwisely and that you have made a bad choice. I see no honor in that. You made your choice—now stick to it and help each other grow. Avoid abandonment at almost all costs.

Oh, what a trip for me marriage has been! I love her more every day and look so forward to growing old (growing old is mandatory—growing up is optional) together. There will be a peace and contentment there known by all too few.

Many theorize about the perfect match. Whether you buy this theory or not, in this arena called marriage, an important essential is something I call sameness.

Yes, you may have differing interests, but lifelong friends share at least some common interests and passions. In my view, the more the better. Best friends work together. Best friends play together. Best friends must be together more often than not. If you love to run, hike, and sleep under the stars, a true soul mate will too. How often I have heard from one spouse or another, "She never golfs with me" or "He just watches TV."

Also, a firm conviction of shared culture, beliefs, values, and expectations simplifies challenges.

Juli, it can be helpful in marriage to read and study. I once read a fantastic book called *His Needs, Her Needs*, which, though I have far to travel, greatly helped me understand my spouse's needs. Also, I once received some very wise counsel and, though I haven't personally had to use it much, I'm told that one secret to a happy marriage is knowing when to be silent. Another is knowing when to be deaf.

Now that you have fallen in love with and married your irresistible best friend, you must develop within you a culture of appreciation for all your partner does for you and your family. Your spouse must become your hobby. It must become a major goal of your life to strengthen your personal relationship and to help your partner feel happy and appreciated. Criticism hurts. It does not heal. Be the person you wish your spouse to become.

Soon, if God so desires, children will join you. What a miracle and blessing children will be in your lives. Yet, all too commonly, one or both best friends begin to make their children the center of their universe. Do not go there.

Yes, children require great sacrifice, time, and energy, but you were lovers before the children came and you will be together alone when they leave home. You must remain passionately in love while they are within your home.

Experience tells me you must continue courting your spouse always. Date often, pay that sitter, plan weekends and trips alone, and your love and marriage will flourish. Ignore this and love often withers and dies.

A woman I visited recently was unsure her marriage would last. She wanted just one thing: for him to hold her hand in public. He refused. What a shame. I reminded him he had made covenants to love and nurture her, and not holding her hand was hypocritical.

In *His Needs, Her Needs*, Willard F. Harley Jr. points out the five needs he believes every wife must meet for her husband and the five needs every husband must meet for his wife in order to make marriage sweet. I will list the needs simply in order of importance to most men and women.

For men they are sexual fulfillment, recreational companionship, attractiveness, domestic support, and admiration.

For women they are affection and kindness, conversation, honesty and openness, financial support, and family commitment.

A friend once gave me a list of 101 ways to tell your wife you love her. Learn and practice gentlemanly ways to show daily affection for your spouse—a phone call, opening doors, appropriate public displays of affection, and such. It is great fun. If any of your best friend's needs go unmet, a void will appear in your relationship.

For those tense times when you have drifted apart, take a long walk. Use humor but beware of hurtful words. These cut deeply and linger long afterward.

How crucial is our decision of who to marry? David O. McKay once said that we would one day have an interview with Father himself. His first question will be, "Did you do everything possible to help your spouse feel joy and happiness?" May we all answer yes.

For those presently struggling, Bruce Springstein wrote a song entitled "If I Should Fall Behind." If one spouse falls behind, forgive and try to help him or her recover. Do not panic about perfection. Too often one spouse will point fingers of blame, which leads too early to the divorce court.

To young people deciding on who to marry, read Doctrine & Covenants 9:7–9, where we are counseled to study it out in our minds and then ask. Research it. When looking for a spouse, the research is half the fun. Make your decision and then take it to your Father in Heaven for that calm assurance within yourself. Then, never look back. Go to your destiny.

I conclude with the hope that we all seek human warmth—a soul mate. I was blessed to find a person whose voice echoed of my own, and I felt a touch that stirs the longings of my heart even when we were apart.

Sure, we have challenges, but I am filled with wonder at the way two lives can blend to weave a pattern to the end.

If you believe some things in life are simply meant to be, then you will know when you have found your soul mate, your destiny.

P.S. Parents are wise, much wiser in most cases than the future bride and groom. Talk to them. Ask their opinion and quietly consider their counsel. They can't say much if you don't ask. Despite former mistakes they may have made, they've been there and they love you.

Do whatever is needed for you to have a meaningful, lasting relationship. Make this happen in your future, where possible, to ever feel truly content. A good friend used to say, "If you aren't happy at home, you aren't happy anywhere."

"Sometimes, in life and marriage, you just need to find the humor in a situation and laugh," I said. "Like the couple who found themselves naked in a pot of hot water the cannibals were brewing. Suddenly the husband began to laugh hysterically. When his wife asked him, 'What's so funny?' he replied with, 'I just peed in their soup!'"

Tune-Up Time

What need or needs can you better meet for your spouse?

How will you improve on each?

* * *

In marriage just accept plain old gender differences. An elderly wife said to her husband, "Just look at the newlyweds next door. He kisses her good-bye every morning and brings flowers each night." When asked why he didn't do that, he responded with, "I hardly even know her."

Chapter Eleven

LDS Makes and Models

My priorities were: first, my own private worship and my faith; second, my wife and family; third, my church service; and fourth, yes fourth, my work.

I believe the LDS Church and its doctrines to be 100 percent true. I do, however, sometimes shudder at our culture. I worry that some of our lifestyle inadvertently may cause part of our pain—even keep people away.

Since eight years of age I have belonged to this church and have known its truths. So you would think I would be able to avoid idolatry—putting false gods before the Lord. Yet busyness, counterfeit praise, money, and such distractions have kept me, from time to time, from really understanding and living the fulness of the truths we have—from seeking Him with all my heart, might, mind, and strength.

We learn in a revelation from God himself (D&C 76:109) that those in a telestial glory are "as innumerable as the stars," and yet we remain distracted.

I first had eyes to see this distractedness when I was bishop. A good friend not of our faith said to me, "I don't have a problem with your doctrines. It's your busy, hurried way of life I just can't do."

This person had known and associated with members of the Church for many years, and this was her observation. She had attended various functions and went on to say, "You even take away the tablecloths while I'm still visiting."

In this person's words, we need to focus our faith more on moral standards and integrity than on busyness and programs.

To encourage us to curb our hurried pace, we're instructed to have fewer but more effective meetings; give Sundays back to families; and to magnify our responsibilities, not our work and time away from home. This takes creativity.

We would do well to spend less time on life's centerpieces. Remember, laminating does not make it true.

I sometimes wonder how much our hectic pace and programs will mean to the Lord if we do not slow our pace, take time to worship and know Him, and follow our inner voices. Too many members of the Church do not even take time to read the scriptues, particularly the one that reminds us, "Be still and know that I am God" (D&C 101:16).

We might be active in the Church and completely miss being active in the gospel. This road leads to trouble.

We thoughtlessly say, "Families come first," when the truth is, God must come first in the truly contented life.

We would do well to improve Sundays by reducing, where possible, meetings and outside distractions to allow us time to rediscover ourselves, family, the needy, and friends. Turn off the TV and consider not answering some phone calls. Use this one day especially to talk, pray, and study. By taking time to really worship alone, you become the master, not the victim, of your week and life.

Though intentions are good, we may forget the proper order of priorities. I recall being asked to become involved with the busy administration of our school. I told the principal, not of our faith, that there was something she must first know. My priorities were: first, my own private worship and my faith; second, my wife and family; third, my church service; and fourth, yes fourth, my work. I was hired.

Too frequently we put busyness before personal worship. I have wondered if the most common unbelief isn't actually that of apparently faithful members who don't really believe and take time to know the Lord.

I have been privileged to serve in three bishoprics. What a gift. I know this requires time. But I learned to be more flexible. I recall a good sister once saying her presidency meeting was held at 5:30 a.m. to accommodate family commitments.

I recently discussed with a friend, not of my faith, how wonderful it is living in our small, predominantly LDS community. He feels it is because the vast majority of people, regardless of their faith, are living good, Christian lives, and he is right. It is not exclusively because Latter-day Saints live here. Too often I fear we lack a degree of multi-faith and multi-cultural acceptance.

Let's hope the joke promulgated in our world is never true of the Saints. Saint Peter was ushering new arrivals into heaven. While passing a certain door, he said, "Shh. The Mormons are in there, and they think they're the only ones up here."

A Church leader I admire once said, "If you do not smell some cigarette smoke in your meetings, you probably aren't doing enough fellowshipping." A friend of mine, who had become less involved and now smoked, heard of this and mustered up the courage to attend. No sooner had he stepped into the foyer than a thoughtless, active member said to him, "Well, I see you still have your bad habit." I know that offenses must be taken and this is no excuse, but my friend turned around and has not returned. Upon hearing this from my less involved friend, I thought, *What stinks most to God? Don't we all stink of something—dishonesty, judgmental behaviors, etc.?*

A Church leader, for who I hold the highest respect, visited the home of a young deacon who had stolen sacred Church funds. Upon entering the home and witnessing this family's poverty, people mattered most, which saved this young leader from a potentially devastating misreading of life. He temporarily disregarded the child's misdemeanor and cared for this family's needs.

Church authorities tell us God loves good people of all faiths. Real Christians care about the entire world. They long to range throughout the world helping others. Mother Teresa, Pope John Paul, and President Hinkley understood this.

The major sin of our day is the same as it was in ancient times—it is the sin against the poor and the destitute. It is in worshipping wealth and wealth's attendant feelings of superiority as others sharing the same streets, and even pews, suffer. Isaiah saw our day and wrote, "Their land also is full of silver and gold . . . neither is there any end of their chariots: Their land is also full of idols; they worship the work of their own hands" (Isaiah 2:7–8).

Latter-day Saints often prosper financially. How we manage the wealth we are blessed with will greatly impact our contentment (D&C 42:33). Do not misinterpret scripture and think prosperity means your life is right before God (2 Nephi 28:21).

A major difference between cultures, faiths, and individuals is simply that they understand differing degrees of correct principles. This ought to humble Church members and make us more grateful for all we can know—not make us more judgmental.

Goodness lies within people. We must not fall prey to the destructive attitude of superiority. Perhaps a king, about to die, said it best when it comes to our possessions: "And ye will seek them [riches] for the intent to do good—to clothe the naked, and to feed the hungry, and to liberate the captive, and administer relief to the sick and the afflicted" (Jacob 2:19).

Maybe instead of using the term *nonmember*, we need to be inclusive and say "not of our faith," and instead of *missionary work*, which conjures up images of some project, I prefer "sincere befriending" no matter the outcomes. All is not well in Zion.

It has been said jokingly that 99 percent of lawyers give the other 1 percent a bad name. I think that when it comes to the LDS people, the reverse is true. About 1 percent give the rest a bad name.

A former bishop actually called this 1 percent of people the Church's 100 percenters. Though well-meaning, they often cause more damage than good. Let me share examples of 100 percenterism.

We talk a lot about self-reliance, as we should. But I don't think God is especially impressed by our self-reliance and one-year supply of food storage.

Obedience to having a one-year supply is important, yes. But caring about neighbors, not our self-reliance, truly impresses God. How we treat others impresses Him. Sharing with the poor and needy impresses Him.

The truth is, no matter how much food storage I have accumulated, in an emergency I will give much away to neighbors in need anyway. These 100 percenters my friend spoke of are territorial. The Lord wants us to love our neighbor over any preparedness.

Well-meaning 100 percenters may think they've done something right by constantly questioning a youth about a mission call, not knowing the rest of the potential elder's painful story.

If I knew the cure for cancer, I would certainly share it generously. We have the cure to this world's discontent—both spiritually and temporally. Share appropriately.

I have few regrets, but, given my former health, I would show more gratitude, give more, love deeper by wiser use of time, and live a life more entirely devoted to lovingly inviting all to come unto God and enjoy His sweet contentment. God bless you on your particular journey.

Our faith is simple: love God and love all others. All people are good. We are not sinners just because we commit sin or fail to complete some task. Brigham Young said we are only sinners if we take joy in sinning. Sinners aren't sorry.

There are some beautiful, life-giving, tank-filling truths many even within the LDS faith may not fully appreciate.

- God is no respecter of persons. He loves us independent of our faith, job, color, or creed.
- God cannot lie. When He says He will forgive us if we demonstrate a broken heart and contrite spirit, He means it.

- Of all God's marvelous attributes, the ones I am personally most grateful for are that He is just and merciful. I don't need or want a God who is simply fair; I will need more—a Savior. Follow the prophets and you'll not be misled. The truth has been returned. Every good part of me says it is so.

We all need to remember, especially the Church members who at present are struggling with a heavy trial, that life is hard; that's just the way it is. We belong to a faith that believes in miracles (Mormon 9), the administering of angels (Moroni 7), and that the heavens are open for business, not busyness.

Continue to believe in old-fashioned Moses-type miracles today. It is profane to think otherwise. What right do we have to limit what God might do?

Never stop believing. Job said, "Though he slay me, yet will I trust" (Job 13:15). Too readily we resign ourselves and fail to boldly importune the Lord (Luke 11:5–11).

Gene R. Cook wrote a marvelous book entitled *Living by the Power of Faith*, which, if you're in the midst of a severe trial, I suggest you read. One way or another, the Lord rescues His disciples but often not until the "fourth watch."

He who created the waters, walked on them, and turned the water to wine, can certainly calm our seas.

True character and commitment to your faith is shown by how you respond to mistreatment. Especially in times when "life's not fair."

Contented, truly grateful people take what they have been given, trusting God knows best.

At some future time, there will be such a sense of completeness and contentment in the world that people will willingly sacrifice all busyness, all praise, all things for God's great purposes. Until that day, may you be trusting and thus experience great contentment in remembering whose you are.

My faith is simple. I believe all the good things are along the path. The path is the gospel of Christ. Avoid or stray from this path at your own great risk.

To all in the midst of trial, Elder James E. Faust has said, "In an unjust world, to survive and even to find happiness and joy, no matter what comes, we must make our stand unequivocally with the Lord. We need to try to be faithful every hour of every day so that our foundation of trust in the Lord will never be shaken. My message is one of hope and council for those who may wonder about the seemingly unfair distribution of pain, suffering, disaster, and heartache in this life."[1] Farewell.

No matter what roads you have or have not taken, never underestimate Father's love and mercy and its enabling power for us, His children.

Notes

1. James E. Faust, "Where Do I Make My Stand?" *Ensign*, Nov. 2004, 18.

Chapter Twelve

All Fellow Drivers

*Never underestimate your own goodness
or the goodness hidden within another person.*

Rodger, Juli, never underestimate your own goodness or the goodness hidden within another person.

I have always believed in the inherent goodness in people. Mr. Rogers of the famous kids' show carried with him a favorite quote. In essence, it said that if you dislike someone, it's simply because you haven't heard their story.

Abe Lincoln similarly believed that if someone is not a friend, you simply do not know that person well enough. I personally have never taught or met anyone that was not likeable in some way. Just keep looking.

Several years ago, our family vacationed in Glacier National Park. All day long the radio had warned of the dreaded Hell's Angels biker gang riding through the valley. Little did I know my wife and I would soon be hugging—yes, hugging—one.

We approached the brow of a hill at sunset, only to find ourselves stopped in the middle of a highway behind many vehicles. It was awesome to see my EMT wife spring into action.

She swung the door open on the minivan, told me to check vehicles for anyone in distress, and then took off running down the road.

A now-crushed van was empty, an unoccupied motorcycle burned, one of the Hell's Angels lay secluded in a nearby ditch as yet undiscovered, and Karen, flashlight in hand, scoured the terrain. A very nervous young police officer radioed something to a rescue helicopter overhead.

The biker's injuries were too severe, and he lost his earth life there beside the road.

The deceased biker's friend, this tough, tatooed man, proceeded to tell how his buddy had called home earlier that day and told his wife (yes, even Hell's Angels have families) that today's ride had been the best of his life and that if he died today he'd die a happy man.

A tear ran down this friend's face as he stretched out his arms to us. He thanked us for trying. We will never forget the night we stood on a lonely stretch of Montana highway, surrounded by members of one of the world's most notorious biker gangs, and were hugged by a Hell's Angel.

Now, what's in this true story for you? First, and essential to your contentment, is that you must never judge people. Only judge situations. Stop talking critically about people.

Second, know there is tremendous good in all people. Look for this because, though often well hidden, it's there.

We spoke earlier of all people literally being children of God. What gives us the right to be anyone's judge and jury?

What sets people above animals is our ability to reason and make choices. Sometimes people exercise this God-given ability unwisely and in opposition to truth. Go easy on yourself and your fellow travelers.

Tune-Up Time

Who do you judge or speak critically of? It might be yourself.

How will you change your language so it's situations, not people, you judge?

* * *

Rodger and Juli, Let me give you a few final tips I have encountered in my trip that I may have omitted, and then I'll go away. Here is your final top ten, upon which I have not extensively commented.

1. Don't keep score. Just enjoy playing the game.
2. Keep in touch with the divine and go off in nature often.

3. Remain passionate about something. Baseball and the Yankees intoxicate me each October. Speaking of baseball—I just learned that the rosary and baseball have something in common: there are 108 beads on one and 108 stitches on the other.
4. People are more valuable than gold or any trappings it may buy, and the small, simple stuff matters.
5. Find yourself some places of perspective. I've used my bathroom, a clump of isolated trees, and our local cemetery. Be still and reflect. Make moments of stillness and reflection part of your song. While I was living in Japan, the Buddhists and Taoists taught me this.
6. Always plan something to look forward to.
7. Laugh. Seek out opportunities for laughter. When we get too serious, our eldest son says, "Suck it up and pull up your pink panties," and then we laugh.
8. When making your living, trust your mind. When making your life, go with the heart.
9. Love your spouse. Make him or her your best friend. Hold each other often. What is essential is also largely invisible.
10. Like reading my little book, remember that this too will pass away.

Rodger and Juli, life will fool us if we aren't careful. Things may not be as they seem.

A local cop sat outside the town pub late one evening. He was set on catching drunk drivers. Around midnight, one man stumbled to his car in an apparent drunken stupor. But instead of driving off, he just sat there. Time passed. All other cars had left when the officer approached the car. To his surprise he found the man completely sober. Upon being questioned, the driver said, "Well, tonight it's my turn to be the decoy."

Epilogue

Arriving at Contentment

Our friends Rodger and Juli are not so different from the rest of us. Hopefully, they'll continue sharing some of life's challenges. I hope all of you realize that contented living begins and ends with accepting we are God's children and through some quiet, regular self-examination.

We all travel similar roads that have their occasional surprises. We travel, uniquely, paths that often surprise and even shock, but though our paths differ, all that really matters in the end is we never quit. Find your way back home.

I know that few will heed my words, but they are true and I know they lead to a more abundant life.

Contented people know that the road of life is not meant to be easy, and they are mature enough to admit and accept this. What they cannot improve they surrender.

Seneca was one of the wise men of ancient Rome. He wrote an essay on happiness and felt that a wise person is content with his lot—that constant complaint certainly never helps any situation.

Just keep driving and remember that road conditions could be worse—adapt. Change speed and direction. God cares most about your current direction.

Sure, you have an excuse to break down now and then. Have a good cry. The world can be like an onion and can be full of hardship. But let your mind dwell less on what you lack and more on what you still have.

Never catch yourself saying, "I'll be happy when my kids are older . . . when I have a new house . . . when I change jobs . . . when I get better . . ." Remember, life is the journey—not the destination. May you find joy and contentment on your trip. The choice forever remains your own.

In the words of one of my Grandma Alston's favorite poems, "Whatever is, is best."

How quickly our time together has passed. Remember these hours and the added light you feel. As difficult as change of speed and direction may be, you are not alone. You have this little book, your reflections, God, and maybe even people who love you. If you need to talk, pick someone you respect and talk to them. Be real and share your pain. This can be very helpful. People need each other.

I know that in the time we spent together you turned onto a more contented road. Time now to get back into traffic, but hopefully it will be at a slower, more purposeful pace. Promise yourself that our culture's roadside distractions will no longer deter you from your meaningful destination—quiet contentment—no matter what happens, because I guarantee that "what" will happen.

Alcoholics Anonymous has a prayer I love. In it one pledges to change those things within their power, and accept what they cannot change.

The Roman philosopher Seneca was falsely accused by Nero. Seneca was ordered to take his own life and could leave no will. Turning to his weeping family, Seneca gently reminded them that they must learn to accept with courage what their circumstances would not allow them to change. Then he left them the best he had to give—the pattern of a contented life. God bless you on your future quests.

All you Rodgers and Julis out there in the thick of life's hectic highway traffic, stay awake at the wheel. Believe it or not, you are steering.

If even one gas station has been pointed out in our time together, I have my pay and my little book was of use. God bless you in your personal trip toward contentment. No more running on empty.

When performing weddings for young people making a new start in life, I would often say to the newlyweds, "May today be the day you love each other least. May today be the least contented day of the rest of your life."

Future Fine Tune-Up Times

In your future, to avoid breakdowns and feeling like you are running on empty, promise yourself you will regularly fill up and annually do some fine-tuning and refueling (maybe each new year or birthday) by reviewing and revisiting gas stations you've been made aware of—keep your tank full. Nurture body and spirit.

One day we all will say good-bye to this life. Just south of my parents' resting place we own a plot of land. Come visit. There will be a bench, birch tree, and a great view of a flat mountain, Old Chief, that is sacred to the native peoples. You talk and I will listen. There, you may even want to try reading my little book. Do not feel sorry for me, because it is in dying that we learn to live. I'll see ya later. I really will.

Love U, B.

"Hand of God" Books

The Bible
The Book of Mormon
The Doctrine and Covenants
Light from Many Lamps edited by Lillian Eichlet Watson
Living by the Power of Faith by Gene R. Cook
If Life Were Easy, It Wouldn't Be Hard by Sheri Dew
Man's Search for Meaning by Victor Frankl
Beginning to End: Rituals of Our Lives by Robert Fulghum
Her Needs, His Needs by Willard F. Harley Jr.
The Lion, the Witch, and the Wardrobe by C. S. Lewis
The Road Less Traveled by Scott Peck
The Giving Tree by Shel Silverstein
Walden by Henry D. Thoreau
The Polar Express by Chris Van Allsburg